THE Smoke Watchers' How-to-Quit Book

THE Smoke Watchers' How-to-Quit Book

Published by
BERNARD GEIS ASSOCIATES

© 1970 by Smoke Watchers International, Inc.

All rights reserved under International
and Pan American Conventions.
Manufactured in the United States of America
Library of Congress Catalog Card Number: 70-97588

FIRST PRINTING

TO
Sandra Costa and Izak Padawer

Smokewatchers International, Inc., expresses its grateful thanks to Bentley Blum and Nicholas Costa, and to Max Gunther for his invaluable assistance in the preparation of this book.

Contents

Introduction   xi
How to Use This Book   xv

PART I
THE TOBACCO HABIT

1. The Tobacco Habit   3
2. Cigarettes and Society   13
3. Cigarettes and the Individual   23

PART II
GATHERING THE FORCES

4. Why Do You Want to Quit?   37
5. The Game of "Cold Turkey"   45
6. ... And Other Games   51
7. Not Stopping but Starting   56

PART III
THE TECHNIQUES OF SUCCESS

8. The Benevolent Pressure Group   63
9. The "Partner" System   74
10. The Problem of Countervailing Pressure   79
11. The Rating Form   85

CONTENTS

12.	Counting and Charting	*107*
13.	The Habit List	*112*
14.	The Smoker's Tic	*130*
15.	Extra Ingredients	*138*
16.	"Withdrawal" Symptoms	*147*
17.	The Smoker and Food	*153*
18.	On Being a Confirmed Nonsmoker	*160*

PART IV
THE CIGARETTE DIET

19.	Making the Commitment	*167*
	Stage I	*172*
	Stage II	*177*
	Stage III	*182*

Introduction

This is a book to help you stop smoking cigarettes. Or, if you prefer, to help you cut down the number you smoke each day. Ideally you should quit entirely—but the choice, of course, is yours to make.

The choice has been yours ever since you began smoking. In fact you have always had three possible courses to choose from: to quit, to cut down, or simply to take no action. Obviously you have already made a partial choice. You have at least tentatively eliminated the last of the three possible courses, the course of no-action, of drifting along, of making or attempting no changes in your life. You are reading this book. Persuaded by any of a hundred conceivable motives, impelled by any of a thousand possible triggering events or circumstances—*for some reason*—you have picked up this book and are taking the time to read it. Perhaps you are reading these first words in a spirit of skepticism; you think you may not finish the book; you aren't sure you have the guts or whatever it takes to overcome your smoking habit; you wonder, indeed, if you really want to. No matter. You are reading the book. You have made some kind of choice. You have taken the first step.

You have done so because, somewhere in either the

INTRODUCTION

forefront or the back of your mind, there is something that urges you to consider making a change in your smoking habit. The something may be strong or weak, loud or muted: anything from a dread of lung cancer to a mild embarrassment about tobacco breath. Whatever it is, it exists and is real and has made you think. You enjoy smoking, and yet . . . you wish you didn't.

Suppose it were possible to switch off your smoking habit effortlessly, like switching off a light. Suppose you could buy a magical pill (you can't, despite what some of the ads seem to imply) that would instantly erase your desire to smoke and erase all memory of ever having smoked—a pill that would transport you blithely back to the position you were in before you tried your first cigarette. Would you want the pill? If your answer is "yes," there is the evidence of that something in your mind. You enjoy smoking but wish you didn't.

The magic pill is not available, of course. So you are still a smoker, perhaps a heavy one. Maybe you've tried to quit or cut down more than once in your life but have always found the effort too great, the craving too strong, the whole experience too unpleasant. Or maybe you've never tried to quit because you doubt your ability to do so, you think you're hooked for life, you fear a battle in which your willpower will be defeated. And yet you are reading this book. You are hoping. . . .

All right. Let's consider the facts coolly. What is this book going to do for you?

It won't make the quit process as easy as taking the mythical switchoff pill. Nobody has yet invented a way to do that. Your wish for tobacco has been developed and nurtured and reinforced over years of habituation. Nothing so long-lived can be exorcized in an hour or a

Introduction

day. This book does not promise any such magical cure.

What it does promise is this: if you read it with care and follow its precepts honestly and faithfully, *it will make the quit or cut-down process far easier than you think.* This book can be your best friend, if you let it.

The book is based on experience. Not theory, not untested gimmicks; *experience.* We don't just think its precepts will work, we don't just hope they'll work. We know they'll work because we've watched them work. Simply and incontrovertibly and absolutely, they work.

The book is based on a program developed over several years and refined by Smoke Watchers International, Inc., an organization devoted exclusively to helping smokers in their battle with tobacco. Thousands of people have now gone through this program; and of every one hundred people who followed the program to completion—including many who had been smoking three or even four packs of cigarettes a day—eighty-six have given up cigarettes entirely and another eleven have cut down to a level of ten cigarettes a day or less. As far as we know, from periodic checkups with these graduates of the program, the changes in almost all cases have been permanent.

We feel good about this. Naturally. Most of us, the executives and group leaders of Smoke Watchers, are ourselves former smokers. Some of us quit in the old days when quitting was often acutely painful. We remember what it was like. We're glad to have made it easier.

"I feel alive again, I feel like a whole woman!" one of our graduates—our Smoke Watchers—once told us. She was a woman of about thirty-five who had been smoking since her teens and had reached the frightening level of

INTRODUCTION

three packs a day. She had tried to quit at least ten times in her life but had always failed miserably. Now she was tobacco's slave no longer. Her complexion had lost its yellowish pallor. Her day's-end fatigue was gone. Her chronic cough was gone. Her teeth were white. Her sex life had become an experience worth having. She had blossomed, she had abruptly come out into the sunshine like a big beautiful butterfly that had spent two decades wrapped in a dingy coccoon. "I'm living!" she kept saying in tones of wonder. "I'm *living!*"

Would you like to live too? Then read on. It won't hurt much. It really won't.

How to Use This Book

The book is divided into four main parts.

The first part is devoted to helping you understand your tobacco habit. The second deals with a preliminary gathering of forces with which to attack the habit. The third explains the actual program of attack.

The fourth part, the Cigarette Diet, is in essence a flexible timetable designed to guide you in using the forces, tools, and techniques presented in the first three parts of the book.

In Parts I, II, and III, the various pieces of information you will need as you go through the Smoke Watchers program are presented as nearly as possible in the order in which you'll need them. However, don't attempt to start yourself through the program as you read these first three parts. Simply read them and digest them. Think of them as a soldier might think of his first months in the army. This is the period in which he receives his basic training, is issued his weapons, and learns how to use them. He doesn't use either the training or the weapons in earnest until a later phase, when he actually goes into battle.

In Part IV, you go into battle. This last part of the book takes you at your own pace through three carefully planned stages from smoker to nonsmoker.

HOW TO USE THIS BOOK

To put it another way, you don't actually commit yourself to the program until you get to the end of Part III. Then, finally, you commit yourself. You go through Part IV stage by stage, using the training and weapons you were given in the first three parts (and, of course, referring to those first three parts as often as necessary). In the end, you are certain to emerge from Part IV as a nonsmoker if you really want to.

Are you ready? Then go on to Part I.

Have a cigarette if you like. You won't be smoking much longer. Or why don't you just skip it? As a gesture of good faith.

THE Smoke Watchers' How-to-Quit Book

PART I

THE TOBACCO HABIT

Alexander the Great remarked once that he never attacked an enemy before understanding him. The dictum applies perfectly to the attack you are about to launch against your smoking habit. One of the major reasons for smokers' failure to defeat the habit is their failure to first understand it thoroughly.

1 🌲 *The Tobacco Habit*

Before you can attack your cigarette habit in a sensible, scientific, and effective way, you've first got to understand it. Thoroughly. The strange fact is that most smokers don't. The typical smoker worries about his habit a lot, castigates himself over it, feels all sorts of unpleasant emotions such as guilt and shame over his failure to defeat it, wonders why he can't, thinks maybe he has less willpower than other people—and, gloomily chasing the elusive subject down the corridors of his mind for the ten-thousandth time, lights another cigarette to comfort himself. He has simply never understood his habit, *really* understood it. At Smoke Watchers we have taken hundreds of smokers through this first step of understanding the habit, and we've watched their faces register surprise and sometimes outright amazement. The habit is actually very easy to understand. But most smokers have apparently never looked at it in the right way, from the right angle. It has been a mystery to them throughout their smoking lives. Many have thought the mystery could be unraveled only by a psychiatrist.

George L. and Mrs. Carol S. were two smokers in their

THE TOBACCO HABIT

mid-thirties who chanced to meet at a Smoke Watchers gathering in Fairfield, Connecticut. Let's examine the separate paths of their lives and see what the similarities were, if any. What made the two paths converge in that room with all those other smokers that night in Fairfield?

George L. had tasted his first cigarette as a teen-ager in the Chicago suburb of Winnetka, Illinois. He was fifteen years old at the time. Like all adolescents, he was having some trouble becoming an adult; the transition from childhood was not easy and was afflicting him with the familiar emotional problems that have troubled teenagers through all the history of human civilization. He had the feeling (probably erroneous) that he was less grown-up, less sophisticated than many of his high-school friends. He was anxious to impress them with his manhood—particularly the girls, and most particularly a gorgeous blonde creature whose name he could not immediately recall when he first began reminiscing for us. What *was* her name? Ah, yes: Jennifer. The beautiful Jennifer has since disappeared into the mists of eternity, but she was important to George at the time.

At a party one warm spring night by the shore of a lake, George was beginning to make time with Jennifer. The group had been swimming in the afternoon and had had a picnic supper, and now as the stars came out, some couples were petting and others were talking about trying to buy some beer from a man they knew. George had taken Jennifer aside. "We were kissing and everything, you know? I was trying to get up the nerve to—well, I actually didn't know what to do next, how to proceed. I was unsure of myself, nervous: a typical kid

The Tobacco Habit

in a typical situation." George was frustrated and relieved at the same time when an older boy came up to him and Jennifer "and made some kind of sexy wisecrack." Jennifer replied with a wisecrack of her own, and George, who couldn't think of anything smart and sophisticated to say, merely stood there and grinned foolishly and felt painfully young.

The older boy was smoking a cigarette. Jennifer (who was probably as relieved as George that the petting session had ended) asked for a cigarette, and the older boy gave her one and then offered the pack to George. "I'd never tried to smoke before, but now I was in kind of a trap. I had to prove my manhood, you see? I felt if I refused that damned cigarette I'd never be able to face Jennifer again. So I took the cigarette and smoked it."

He tried to smoke it the way he'd seen Humphrey Bogart do it in the movies. He didn't inhale but he tried to ape all the other Bogart mannerisms. Humphrey Bogart was one of the cigarette industry's leading salesmen. He didn't intend to be, but that is what he was. He could make a minor dramatic episode out of lighting a cigarette. Sometimes he would light one and then give it to Lauren Bacall, and the audience was encouraged to presume that the next stop was bed. The act of smoking a cigarette had all the qualities of sexual foreplay, and the movie industry (which in those days was not allowed to show real sex except in its most remotely symbolic forms) made the most of this allowable kind of sex-but-not-sex. Impressionable youngsters might have been harmed much less if the actor and actress had been shown naked in bed together, but public values are not always entirely sensible and this was the way the nation wanted it. Humphrey Bogart, smoking a cigarette, was all man: tough, hardboiled, sophisticated, unquestionably male, the archetype of modern urban manhood.

And so George L. smoked his first cigarette and tried to look like a hardboiled private eye and hoped Jennifer was impressed. Though he didn't inhale, the smoke made him cough and burned his mouth and nose and made his eyes water. His body was trying to tell him something, but of course he paid no attention. Over the next few months he practiced smoking in front of mirrors until he got the hang of it. From then on, throughout his adolescence, he smoked whenever he wanted to look and feel like an adult male.

At about the same time George L. was going through this not unusual adventure, the girl who would later become Mrs. Carol S. was also learning to smoke. Like George, she tried her first cigarette in high school. She was with a group of four girls in a car in a movie parking lot. One of the girls had a pack of cigarettes that she had bought from a coin-operated machine, and she suggested that they all try smoking. "There was a lot of giggling," Carol recalled as she tried to reconstruct the episode for us, "and a lot of hesitating. I don't think any one of us really wanted to do it. But somehow the whole thing turned into a dare. You know how high-school girls are. They hate to be different. They've got to be one of the bunch. Being a member of a group is a desperately important thing at that age. I didn't want to get ostracized from the group, even for one silly night. So I went along with the dare and smoked."

She was then a senior in high school. She smoked

about four cigarettes a week from then until graduation, never really enjoying the act, smoking merely to maintain what she felt was her position in the group— "and also, I guess, using cigarettes as a way of secretly defying the grown-up world. I got along well with my parents and the teachers in school and other adults, but—well, you know how it is with a kid. I felt I was more of an adult than they thought. I had to rebel in some quiet way. Every kid does, I suppose. Smoking that one cigarette in back of the movies or down at the local soda store every Saturday night: that was my way of defying adults and showing I had my own life and could run it by myself. It seemed like a harmless kind of defiance at the time. After all, I asked myself, who am I hurting?"

But she didn't really like cigarettes. When summer vacation arrived that year, her high-school gang dispersed. She did not smoke all summer, felt no need or even a remote wish to smoke. Then she went to college: Gettysburg College in Pennsylvania. Like all or almost all college girls, she now considered herself to have crossed the threshold into full adulthood. She and other girls in the dorms were no longer living with their parents; they were on their own, independent; the world had now issued each a license to chart her own course through life. Many girls in the dorms smoked. They smoked as they talked of their adult concerns: sex, marriage, careers, religion, politics. It was an exhilarating experience to be a full-fledged adult at last, and smoking somehow seemed to be part of the experience, tangled up with it in ways that nobody ever stopped to explain but that seemed not to need explanation. Smoking simply existed, that was all. It was there. It was something you did.

THE TOBACCO HABIT

Carol began to smoke again, very lightly, in her sophomore year. At first she smoked only among other girls in the dorm or on dates at night, still not particularly enjoying the smoke itself but enjoying the sense of adult companionship that seemed to go along with it. In the beginning, the sense of companionship (the "groupness," she called it) simply existed side-by-side with the smoking. Later, the smoking seemed to *create* the sense of fellowship, the feeling of being in the group. "Gradually I got to a point where I felt ill at ease among people if I didn't have a cigarette. The cigarette gave me a feeling of security, kind of. I didn't analyze what was happening at the time, of course. I guess nobody does. I simply drifted along and let cigarettes get more and more tangled up with my life."

Meanwhile, George L. had been in and out of the U.S. Navy and was starting his career as an accountant. Cigarette-smoking had started for him as an act to prove his manhood. In the Navy he had gradually increased his cigarette consumption, but this was not because he felt a growing need to prove himself a man. Perhaps this need or its vestiges still existed somewhere in his subconscious mind, but it was not an overt need any more as it had been in his adolescence. He knew he was a man and so did everybody else. He had grown into a muscular six-footer, impressively bright, well supplied with women friends who gave him repeated assurance of his virility. It was not necessary to smoke before them —as he had felt in the case of Jennifer—in order to prove himself; nor was it necessary to smoke before his Navy

The Tobacco Habit

shipmates. He knew this. And yet he smoked more each year.

For smoking had now become a habit. At first he had smoked specifically to regain his honor as a man when he felt it was threatened; then he had smoked automatically in mixed groups to defend his honor before it was threatened; then he had smoked in all groups; then he had smoked whenever he was nervous or worried about anything, in any situation; and finally he had drifted into the pattern of smoking all day long. There was no longer a particular reason for pulling out any particular cigarette in the long day's chain. Each cigarette seemed to give him some vague comfort even when there was no specific problem that he needed to be comforted about. Smoking had become little more than a set of half-voluntary reflex actions: one hand into his shirt pocket for the cigarette pack, the other hand into his pants pocket for a lighter; *click-click* . . . a deep drag . . . *Ah-h-h!* Every hour. Every half-hour. Every twenty minutes.

By the time he was thirty and married and making plans to form his own public-accounting firm, George L. was smoking well over two packs of cigarettes a day, and he was worried about it. He detected some faintly frightening signs of failure in his once robust body. He could not walk up one flight of stairs without panting. He had a chronic cough. He was so fatigued at the end of a two-pack day that he was even losing interest in sex. When he went to bed at night with his wife he was usually too tired to do more than groan and roll over and fall asleep and—his smoke-irritated respiratory passages being clogged with mucus—snore. None of this was contributing to the success of his marriage. The irony of it gave him a sour and bitter amusement: he had started smoking because of sex, and now he was quitting sex because of smoking.

On three separate occasions he tried to give up cigarettes. The longest he was able to go without them was a period of four days. "I'd always feel great the first day when I'd decide to quit," he told us. "I'd be full of enthusiasm, proud of myself—you know? I'd look at all the other guys smoking on the train or around the office and I'd think, 'Those lily-livered bastards, they're weak, weak, weak!' But on the second day I'd wake up and think, 'Oh Christ, how am I going to get through another day without cigarettes? What'll I do with myself?' And the craving would get worse and worse, and finally I'd think, 'Well, I'll just have one with my morning coffee.' And then I'd have another, and another, and pretty soon I'd admit to myself that I'd failed again."

Carol similarly found herself hooked on cigarettes by the time she got out of college. She had started smoking in groups, but now she was smoking when alone as well. "I had this feeling that cigarettes helped me think. I'd smoke when I was reading or writing my reports and essays in college. It seemed like an adult kind of thing to do, if you know what I mean. It made life seem—well, serious. It helped me take myself seriously, made me feel important. I thought I could stop smoking any time I wanted to, but of course I was wrong."

Carol married at the age of twenty-four. Her husband was a very heavy smoker, sometimes reaching the level of three packs a day. Soon after their first child was born, he developed a peptic ulcer. His doctor ordered

The Tobacco Habit

him flatly to stop smoking, pointing out that his life could conceivably depend on whether he did or not. Carol, badly scared, made a pact with her husband: they would stop smoking together.

"It was a farce," Carol recalled later. "I guess we both honored our pact on the first day or two. But we had our separate lives to lead. He'd go to his job every morning and I'd be home with the baby. On the afternoon of the second day, I guess it was, or maybe the third, I couldn't stand the craving any longer. So I put the baby in his carriage and walked six or seven blocks to a drugstore and bought a pack of cigarettes. I sat at the lunch counter, bought a cup of coffee, and lit up. Oh, it was heaven! When I walked out of the drugstore I was disgusted with myself, so I threw the pack away. But I was back twice the next day, and the day after that I was smoking in front of open windows at home, with a fan going so my husband wouldn't smell the smoke that night. I was ashamed of myself, but I didn't feel there was anything I could do about it. Then, that weekend, my husband—bless him!—admitted to me that he had broken the pact too. He'd been smoking on his job. I fell into his arms and cried. I was happy but sad too. The habit had us both trapped."

George L.'s smoking and his worries about smoking continued to increase. When he was thirty-four a chest X-ray showed a faint spot on his right lung. In a retake of the X-ray picture, the spot failed to show up. "It was just a photographic error," the doctor told him. "All the same, I'd like to think this has scared you a little. You really ought to stop smoking," he added. George was

THE TOBACCO HABIT

scared, all right. "I tell you, I was scared witless." He tried once again to quit smoking. But he couldn't make it.

Carol S.'s husband was rushed to a hospital one night with his ulcer hemorrhaging. He could not smoke in the hospital, but as soon as he was convalescing at home he was smoking again. Carol determined to give up cigarettes herself and encourage him to follow. But she lasted only a day and a half.

George L. and Mrs. Carol S. both ended at a Smoke Watchers meeting. They needed help. Neither understood the tobacco habit.

2 ❦ *Cigarettes and Society*

There were many similarities in the smoking histories of George L. and Mrs. Carol S. One similarity stands out above all the others. It is overwhelmingly important. For reasons that will become apparent later, you should think about it hard and study the relationship it bears to your own smoking history.

It is this: George and Carol both started smoking because of social pressures.

They did not start because they felt some inner craving for a cigarette, some genetically established need such as the need for a mother's love or food or sex. The wish to smoke was not born in them. If either of them, as a teen-ager, had been stranded on a tropical island with a whole shipload of cigarettes, neither would have smoked. There would have been no reason to do so, no pressure, no urge. Each, perhaps, might conceivably have tried one cigarette out of curiosity, just to see what this odd white cylinder was and what its effects were. But neither would have enjoyed those first few puffs and neither would ever have smoked again.

THE TOBACCO HABIT

To become a smoker, you must first learn to like cigarettes. Nobody ever liked the first one he tried. George did not like his first cigarette, but he liked the feeling of manhood it gave him. Carol found her first one distinctly unpleasant, but she would have found exclusion from her peer group still more upleasant—or so she felt at the time. Each gradually learned to like smoking because each felt socially pressured into repeated acts of smoking. What was unpleasant at first gradually became tolerable, then became vaguely pleasant, and finally became a habit.

What is the nature of these social pressures? How has it happened that a civilized society, in most respects a rational and highly successful one, harbors within its complex machinery a set of inimical and even suicidal pressures? Historically, societies have lived, improved, and become successful because of pressures operating in the direction of success: that is, each individual has felt compelled, in general, to do what will improve his own lot and that of the society as a whole. Yet here we are engulfed in the social compulsion to smoke—a compulsion to do something that will certainly not improve our lot or society's, will probably damage our health, and may lead to our premature death. What's it all about? Where did this mad, mad anomaly come from? Why hasn't a sensible society wiped it out? If you understand the answers to these questions, you'll begin to develop a necessary insight into your own smoking habit.

Sir Walter Raleigh is generally credited with having introduced tobacco to Western civilization some time

Cigarettes and Society

around 1600, but this is probably not quite true. Many European explorers and merchants in the mid-1500s watched the natives of both North and South America smoking tobacco in pipes or cigars. A Dutch merchant once asked an Indian near what is now Chicago why he smoked, what pleasure he got out of it. "I do not know," the Indian replied. "My father smoked tobacco, and so did his father before him. All the males of my tribe smoke. Therefore, I smoke." The Dutch merchant went away chuckling over the foolishness of it. He did not dream that the powerful, aggressive, hugely successful Western civilization that he represented would one day adopt the same attitude and be forced to answer the same question in roughly the same way.

A French traveler, André Thevet, brought some tobacco seed home from Brazil in 1556 and raised a tobacco crop in a field near Paris. He rolled the dried leaves into cigars and claimed to enjoy them. Among his friends was Jean Nicot, a diplomat and adventurer with an inquiring mind and an entrepreneur's habit of looking for situations in which money could be made. Nicot knew that many members of the French court at the time—indeed, of most European courts—were bored and restless, searching for new thrills and new ways to occupy time. He introduced tobacco-smoking to the French nobility, and the intriguing idea caught on and spread into other countries. Thevet's tobacco field (in which Nicot had carefully purchased a large interest) sold out year after year. Soon it became profitable to import tobacco from America, where the weed grew bigger and better. By the time Nicot died, the tobacco trade was growing steadily, and grateful merchants had seen to it that Nicot's name would not be forgotten. The common tobacco plant had been named after him: genus *Nicotiana*. In later years, Nicot would also give his name posthumously to an ingredient of tobacco smoke, nicotine.

It would have been better for the world if Nicot's inquisitive eye and sharp mind had been turned to other fields of endeavor.

Throughout the seventeenth century, tobacco-smoking was a kind of status-seeking gambit among educated and cultured Europeans, or those who fancied themselves as such. It occupied roughly the same niche in that society as, say, marijuana-smoking and underground-movie-going do in our society today. It was something you did if you wanted to show how avant-garde you were. It had intellectual snob appeal. Intellectuals, in fact, claimed that the smoke helped them think. The "azure vapours" obviously would not do any good for the great mass of common men, who (in the intellectuals' view) did not need to think and weren't capable of thinking in any case.

Anything with that much snob appeal would naturally attract those against whom the snobbery was directed. "Common" men wanted to smoke tobacco too, just to show that they were as intellectual as anybody else. (In the same way, modern suburbanites smoke pot and visit underground movies to show that they are more With It than their neighbors.) The use of tobacco grew rapidly. Farmers in Virginia exported 18 million pounds of the weed in 1700, 40 million in 1750, and 123 million in 1800. Tobacco, like a huge octopus, was gradually extending and tightening its grip on the civilized world.

Throughout all this time, there was never any serious medical objection to the weed. There were medically oriented objections, but they were mostly based on religious or moral considerations and were generally dismissed as quackery—and were, in fact, quackery. Nobody really studied the physical effects of tobacco-smoking. Fundamentalist religious groups, which seemed to object to anything that was fun, including sex, tried to convince everybody that smoking caused warts, epileptic fits, and other physiological problems—not to mention its role in the eternal damnation of the soul. It is now known for certain, of course, that smoking does indeed cause disease. But the anti-smoking campaigns of earlier centuries were not based on reliable evidence and were quite properly laughed at by the general smoking public. When reliable and believable evidence was at last produced early in the twentieth century, smokers still had the traditional and understandable tendency to ridicule such evidence as just another flurry of pseudo-religious nonsense: mere fire-and-brimstone preaching by bluenosed neurotics who didn't know how to have fun and hated everybody who did. Thus it took a long time for the real evidence, the reliable evidence, to get itself sold.

Meanwhile the tobacco industry was making a fortune. Cigarettes (a French word meaning "little cigars") had been invented in the seventeenth century but remained obscure until early in this century. They became popular suddenly. They were cheap, neat, easy to carry around, easy to light, easy to handle. During and right after the First World War, "emancipated" women (as they called themselves) began to smoke along with men. The same intellectual-cultural snob appeal that had made tobacco itself attractive in earlier centuries now served to make cigarettes attractive to women.

THE TOBACCO HABIT

Tobacco now had a grip on almost the entire world. Cigarettes by the millions were sold in every Western nation and most Eastern nations as well. Not much is known about the tobacco industries of modern Russia and China, but casual observation indicates that the Russians, at least, smoke about as many cigarettes per capita as we do (and are equally worried about the fact). Large numbers of Chinese cannot afford cigarettes, but among urban and professional Chinese who have the required money and the access to tobacco stores, smoking is evidently just as common as in New York or Paris.

While thus spreading through the civilized world, tobacco picked up and gradually accumulated new sociological connotations as societies used it and absorbed it into their thinking and shaped their attitudes around it. Tobacco began its modern career as a plaything of European nobility. Then it became a status symbol of those who wished to be thought cultured, intellectually adventurous. Gradually, then, it became a symbol of sophistication, of urbanity. A man could smoke to convince himself and (he hoped) others that he was neither a hayseed nor an uninteresting, inhibited, rigidly conforming bourgeois. He was worldly-wise, he knew his way around.

For adolescents and for adults still concerned about their own maturity, smoking became a symbol of adulthood. Cigarette in hand, one could feel older, wiser, more able to cope with life and its problems. This connotation gradually spread like an inkblot into the area of sex. If a cigarette could make a boy or girl feel more

Cigarettes and Society

adult, it could also make the smoker feel and look more mature and experienced sexually. An adventurous, convention-be-damned spirit came to be associated with smoking—particularly in the case of women, who historically adopted the cigarette habit later than men. Earlier in this century, women who smoked were also likely to be those who defied convention in other ways. They were esoteric poetesses, members of oddball political groups, advocates of what was reverently called Free Love. The idea gradually grew that a woman who smoked was probably adventurous sexually as well. The movies latched onto this convenient bit of symbolism long ago and have never let go of it. In the movies all prostitutes, lady spies, rich men's mistresses, delinquent teen-age girls, lady criminals, private eyes' girlfriends, and adulteresses smoke. Nice old ladies, sweet young mothers, and understanding schoolteachers don't smoke. A girl who wishes to enhance her sexiness is thus encouraged to believe she can do so by smoking.

Still other connotations were added to the sociological complex, one by one. Smoking became an act of companionship. Offering a man a cigarette became a gesture of friendship. It is a cheap gesture, since cigarettes even now cost only about 2¢ apiece. The offered cigarette tells the recipient, "I want to be your friend. I don't want to give you an expensive gift because that would seem like an attempt to buy you. Therefore I offer you this inexpensive token of my goodwill." The act of lighting another man's cigarette is a similar gesture.

For a man, lighting a woman's cigarette (or giving her one and then lighting it) can be the opening move of a courtship. One traditional way for a woman to gain a man's attention—in a cocktail lounge, for instance—

is to take out a cigarette and ask him for a light. Later in their relationship, he will light her cigarette as a gesture of courtesy, in the same way as he opens doors for her or helps her on with her coat.

Thus deeply has tobacoo burrowed its way into our culture. It is buried so deeply, intertwined so thoroughly with our cultural roots, that it has in fact become a part of the culture. Smoking is not like eating an ice-cream cone or going swimming or gazing at the stars, which each individual can elect to do or not do as he sees fit, without great pressures upon him in either direction. Our very culture urges us to start smoking and, once started, to continue. Is it any wonder that millions of people like George L. and Mrs. Carol S. are smokers? Is it any wonder that *you* are one?

On top of all these social pressures, consider one other kind of external pressure—perhaps the most powerful of all. This is the pressure exerted by the tobacco industry.

The tobacco industry is absolutely enormous. The world production of tobacco in 1967 was over 10 billion pounds, of which some 2½ billion pounds came from the United States. In that year, American companies produced 580 billion cigarettes—an all-time record—and Americans smoked 511 billion of them. (It was estimated that in 1967 the cigarette-consumption total was swelled by about a million young people who started smoking for the first time during the year. It was also estimated that the total was diminished somewhat by the fact that 300,000 Americans died prematurely during the year as a result of having smoked.)

Cigarettes and Society

This huge industry does not intend to sit quietly and watch everybody quit smoking. And, though it frequently utters pious claims to the contrary, it will certainly continue its efforts to recruit a million or more new customers each year. At the first World Conference on Smoking and Health, held in New York in 1967, the late Senator Robert F. Kennedy told delegates that the tobacco industry spends nearly $300 million a year in this country on television, radio, and newspaper advertising. The highest-priced, cleverest ad agencies in the world are involved in this monumental pro-smoking campaign. To resist the colossal force of it is not easy.

Another man who attended the 1967 World Conference was Emerson Foote, who had once been president of a leading ad agency. He had resigned because of the agency's involvement in cigarette advertising. In his view, it was at best a distasteful business for the agency to be in and at worst an immoral one. Other officers of the agency, which earned several million dollars a year from its cigarette account, did not agree. Emerson Foote told the conference delegates that his former agency and others work "in all media to represent cigarette smoking as a pleasurable, relaxing and adult practice. . . . Whatever effect this exposure to cigarette advertising may have on adults, its effect on teen-agers verges on the catastrophic. . . ."

The cigarette commercials are highly compelling. Some years ago the tobacco industry voluntarily agreed not to present advertising in which very young smokers were pictured. The industry then patted itself on the back for this display of social conscience. But the gesture was a hollow one. It's true that the smokers we see in TV commercials and on the back covers of magazines are plainly adults; they seem in general to be somewhere in the twenty-five to thirty-five age bracket. But they are carefully presented as the adults we all want to be, our cultural heroes and heroines. They are all good-looking, sophisticated, sure of themselves, usually somewhere in the upper or upper-middle income bracket (they all seem to live on huge country estates). They are adults who are plainly enjoying successful careers and rewarding love lives. They appreciate art, music, and literature. They think a lot. They are in the 140-plus I.Q. range. Smoking is an inextricable part of their wide, wide, glamorous world.

Do you wonder why you're a smoker? Do you begin to see now why it has been so hard for you to quit?

3 🌲 *Cigarettes and the Individual*

Social pressures started you smoking and have since played a major role in making you continue. But what of the forces inside you? What are they? How do they operate? What is this sinister magic, unseen, elusive, that makes you reach eternally for another cigarette even when you are by yourself?

There is no doubt that this internal force exists. A young father named Fred J. once told Smoke Watchers of a bad and lonely time when he came face-to-face with it. "I'd figured out part of the truth about smoking," he told us. "I'd seen that social pressures played a big part. I guess I figured that, if I could get away from everybody and everything for a while, it would be easy to give up cigarettes. But I didn't see the whole truth."

His plan was to go away somewhere by himself for a week. He had heard from friends who were former smokers that the first few days of the quit process are the hardest. "If you can get through one week," a business colleague had told him, "you've got it just about licked. One week: that's all. A week of misery, and you're free for life."

Fred mulled this over for a long time. He had tried to quit smoking several times before and had found that the first few days were, indeed, hard. So hard, in fact, that he had not been able to endure them. Tobacco had defeated him every time on the second day.

He began to think about social pressures. He noticed that he smoked more heavily on the busier days at the office (he was an assistant editor of a small monthly magazine), at bridge games (he was an expert player, holder of several Master's points), at parties, and in general at the more peopled junctures of his life. He thought: "People, society, the tension of this overpopulated life: that's what does it. If I can get away from everybody, away from the whole rush and roar, I'll make it, I'll make it!"

It wasn't that Fred J. disliked people or disliked his life. He was no misfit in twentieth-century urban America. He found his life thoroughly enjoyable and stimulating—was, in fact, gregarious to a high degree. But he recognized that his smoking had something to do with other people, and this was the clue he seized upon. He had an analytical mind. The trouble was, like many or perhaps most smokers seeking to escape the habit, he didn't carry his analysis far enough or deep enough.

While he was thinking these thoughts, an apparently heaven-sent opportunity suddenly arose to put his thoughts to the test. The managing editor of his magazine asked him to tackle a special editing assignment. "Take all of next week to do it," the managing editor said. "Take your phone off the hook and lock yourself up someplace with the job. You can do it at home if you want. Just show up next Friday with the job done."

This was it! Fred talked the matter over with his wife,

Cigarettes and the Individual

who was a nonsmoker and who had long been gently urging Fred to quit. They owned a small summer cabin on a lake three hours' drive away. At this season, mid-autumn, the lake would be virtually deserted. The cabin had an electric heater that would warm its small space adequately unless the fall days suddenly turned winter-cold, which was not yet likely. Fred and his wife decided that he should spend the week at the cabin. With his editing job. Without his cigarettes.

Before he started the long drive, he stood next to his car and smoked a cigarette, thinking, *This will be the last one.*

On second thought, he decided that it would be the next-to-last. The long drive would be boring and fatiguing. He had long been in the habit of smoking in cars to relieve boredom and (he told himself) keep awake. He decided that he would smoke one cigarette at the halfway point of the route.

He emptied all but one cigarette from his pack and threw the others away.

He did not enjoy the drive. He couldn't wait until he reached the halfway mark. When he had driven about a third of the way he thought, *Why torture myself?* He smoked the cigarette then and there. It seemed easier to do it that way. From here on, he told himself, the only willpower required would be that of not pulling into a gas station to buy more cigarettes.

He made it to the cabin just as dusk was falling. He brewed some coffee, sipped it, and looked out over the lonesome lake. Not one human being was in sight. The calm water reflected a magnificent pink and purple sky. The only sound Fred could hear was the hushed whisper of a breeze in the great hemlocks that surrounded the cabin. "I don't think I'd ever known such tranquility," Fred recalled later. "Perfect peace. Somewhere out there the world was pell-melling along, people were running for trains and drinking and jabbering at each other and worrying and smoking. But I was all alone. No pressure and no cigarettes."

He felt enormously exhilarated, brimming with new confidence. Why, he didn't even want a cigarette! He was going to make it!

He went to bed early and arose early the next morning. He missed the cigarette that wasn't there with his morning coffee. He thought, *Well, the day's first drag was always the best. I won't miss the others so much.*

Unfortunately, he did. He sat down at a table to begin his editing work. After a quarter of an hour he had to stand up and go outside and walk among the hemlocks. He wanted a cigarette badly.

He thought, *I've got to stop thinking about cigarettes.* He sat down at the table again, determined to concentrate the whole energy of his mind on the work. For a while he was successful. He became absorbed in the job. He worked steadily for nearly an hour. Then, coming to a stopping point, he leaned back in his chair and automatically reached into his shirt pocket for a cigarette.

And was jolted back to reality.

The work went very slowly for the rest of the day. He took frequent breaks, once walking all the way around the lake, a distance of four miles. He went to bed early again. *The only time quitting doesn't bother you,* he thought, *is when you're asleep.*

The next morning he got up, drank a cup of coffee that he didn't enjoy, and thought about all the work he

Cigarettes and the Individual

should have got done the day before but hadn't. The job had to be finished by Friday. How could he possibly finish in this miserable, nervous state?

He climbed into his car, drove to the nearest gas station, and bought a pack of cigarettes.

. . .

Is it an addiction? A physical addiction, something like the hook of hard narcotics?

Doctors don't quite agree on this point. Some believe there may be a physically addictive property in nicotine or some other, perhaps yet undiscovered, ingredient of inhaled tobacco smoke. Others say the entire problem is psychological in nature, not physical. In any case, the argument is neither very heated nor very important. All doctors agree that, if there is a physically addictive component in the action of smoke on the human mind and body, this physical component is extremely weak.

As a matter of fact, medical men don't even agree on the definition of "addiction." In general, however, a thoroughgoing physical addiction is usually thought of as having two main characteristics:

(1) The addict needs ever larger doses of the addicting substance in order to satisfy his craving. Thus a heroin addict may begin by injecting minor doses into his buttock or arm muscle and end by pumping massive doses into his femoral artery—"mainlining," as it's called. He progresses from one fix a week to one or more a day, the terminal condition being one in which he must maintain a certain concentration of the drug in his system all day long, injecting each new dose before the old one's effects have worn off. He may need so much of the drug that he ultimately drugs himself to death.

THE TOBACCO HABIT

Similarly, an alcoholic begins by getting drunk on random occasions, then regularly, then at least once a day, and finally all day. Cigarette smoking exhibits this "evermore" characteristic to some extent, but not commonly to a severe extent. The typical smoker, throughout his life, meanders up and down from heavier smoking to lighter smoking. He may smoke a lot one week or one day, less the next week. There is apparently no fixed or rising minimum concentration of chemical substances that his body requires him to maintain.

(2) The addict suffers severe illness or even death if he stops supplying his body with the addicting substance. The substance, in other words, has become so inextricably tangled with his body chemistry that his body *requires it physically*. No such severe withdrawal symptoms have ever been observed in anybody who stopped smoking. There are certain physical withdrawal symptoms, it's true (as we'll discuss later), but they are so mild that they can't be called anything worse than irritating. They are less painful than a cold or a mild case of poison ivy, even for the heaviest smokers.

Thus, physical addiction is only a very minor part of your smoking complex, and for all practical purposes you can forget about it. Doctors have experimented with various chemicals to help smokers quit, but the results of these experiments show—without exception—that the most you can expect from any anti-smoking drug is a very temporary and very minor kind of help. For example:

• *Nicotine* is one of the active ingredients in tobacco smoke, and doctors have tried giving smokers this

Cigarettes and the Individual

chemical by pill or injection. The experimenters hoped this might alleviate or at least dull the tobacco craving by saturating the smoker's body with the active drug he formerly obtained by inhaling smoke. The idea sounds promising—but unfortunately it doesn't work. In a paper on the subject, Dr. Borje Ejrup of the New York Hospital–Cornell Medical Center recently reported: "Nicotine does not give any pleasurable effect in itself. It is an emetic. (In excess, it produces nausea.) Neither do the other chemicals in tobacco give pleasure by themselves."

The pleasurable effect, in other words, comes from the *act of smoking*, not from chemical changes produced in the body by the ingredients of the smoke. This is exactly the opposite of the situation that obtains with such drugs as heroin. A heroin-user takes the drug by injecting it into himself. The act of injecting is not pleasurable; in fact it can be acutely painful if the needle is dull or the body area is bruised or inflamed by too many previous injections. In this case, the user gets his pleasure from the chemical changes that take place in his body *after* the injection. Unlike the smoker's habit, the heroin-user's habit is based on a physical addiction.

- *Lobeline hydrochloride* is another drug that once looked promising to experimenters. It is a drug that, when mixed in the body with nicotine, produces nausea and other unpleasant physical reactions. If you've been given an injection of thirty to sixty milligrams of lobeline, you can't smoke much for the next twelve to twenty-four hours because your body can't absorb the nicotine. If you do smoke, you get sick.

This sounds like a good way to give up smoking. However, it doesn't work. The wish to smoke remains as strong as it ever was. Several clinics around the world have tried to help people break the habit by means of daily lobeline injections, and the results have always been the same.

(1) After the second or third day, more than half the patients would fail to turn up at the clinic for their injections. They wanted to go on smoking. They wanted no more of the drug that prevented smoking. It hadn't helped them at all.

(2) The rest of the patients would stick with the lobeline course to the bitter end—and then, in most cases, would immediately start smoking again. A lobeline course can't be continued much longer than two weeks because of unpleasant and possibly dangerous side effects from the drug. Thus, the best it can do is force a two-week hiatus in your smoking career. There are no long-term effects. Twenty-four hours after your last lobeline shot, you're right back where you started. Unless some other kind of anti-smoking therapy accompanies the lobeline, the drug does no good whatever. As one smoker who tried it reported to us: "I might as well have saved my money. Lobeline might be useful if some other kind of nonsmoking therapy went along with it—but if that 'other' therapy was good and if it did most of the work, why bother with lobeline at all? The only things I got out of it were a dent in my bank account and a ten-day upset stomach."

- *Tranquilizers* can also help a little, but not much. Sometimes, in fact, they're worse than useless. The idea

Cigarettes and the Individual

of taking them is to ease the nervousness, irritability, and vague discomfort of the recent quitter. But the hoped-for effects don't always materialize.

"I thought I could tranquilize myself away from cigarettes," one forty-seven-year-old woman told us. "I figured, 'If smoking is a nervous habit, then the way to stop is to deaden your nerves.' I told myself, 'I'll get so tranquil and dreamy and happy that I won't miss cigarettes at all.' Well, let me tell you what happened. I dosed myself up on tranquilizers one morning. Pretty soon I got so tranquil that I wasn't worried about the dangers of smoking any more. All my willpower seemed to dissolve. I smoked happily all day, and at the end of the day it turned out I'd smoked more than on any normal day before I ever decided to quit."

. . .

No, your habit cannot be attacked with chemicals, because it is not based on physical effects. It is what some medical men call a psychological, as against physical, addiction.

Social pressures made you start smoking and made you continue until you had acquired a taste for cigarette smoke. You didn't like the smoke at first, but after sufficient practice you got to like it. You became used to having it around. Eventually you became habituated to it. You became so used to having it around that your life would have seemed empty without it.

Conceivably, you could have become habituated to some other pleasurable but harmful activity. Cigarette smoking, however, tends to become a habit much more easily and quickly than most other activities.

Unlike food, tobacco smoke doesn't fill you up. There

are people who are compulsive eaters. They eat until it literally hurts. Most of us, though we may often eat more than we really should, keep our eating within reasonable bounds because there are *immediate, painful* effects from overeating. Not so from smoking.

Unlike alcohol, tobacco smoke doesn't *immediately, tangibly, and visibly* affect your ability to carry on your normal daily affairs. Alcohol gives us very quick and powerful and insistent warning signs when we are indulging in it too much—and, as a result, most of us approach it with caution and use it moderately. Tobacco gives its warnings much more subtly and over a much longer period of time.

Because tobacco doesn't give immediate and visible warnings, society long ago accepted it as permissible for adults—and you, once you had started smoking, accepted it as permissible for yourself. There was no pain, no quickly apparent damage to your health, no apparent diminution of your capacity to walk, talk, perform your job. It was a very easy habit to slide into.

And so you slid. You got so used to cigarettes that your life and thoughts became oriented around them. Cigarettes became seemingly fixed into your daily activities; you reached for your pack automatically, without really thinking, at certain times and in certain kinds of situations every day, every week. A cigarette had to be your companion at each of these times or you had a feeling of something missing. In effect (as we'll discuss later), each cigarette became a habit by itself—a subhabit within the general smoking habit.

"I always had to have a cigarette with coffee," one Smoke Watcher told us. "Without a cigarette, coffee wasn't coffee."

Cigarettes and the Individual

As soon as a cup of coffee was set down before him, he reached for cigarettes automatically, almost like some kind of machine that had been programed to follow a set sequence of motions in the presence of coffee. A laboratory rat can be trained to react in the same blind, unthinking way to a stimulus. The smoker had trained himself to react to the stimulus of coffee by smoking. The coffee cigarette was a sub-habit.

Other smokers react to other stimuli, and so form other sub-habits. There are probably as many varieties of stimuli as there are smokers. Some samples taken from Smoke Watchers' files:

A housewife: "I always smoked when I finished something, whether it was some chore like washing the dishes or some pleasant activity like planting flowers. If I had a long job to do, I'd mentally divide it into segments and have a cigarette after the first segment, and another after the next, and so on. My whole day was dominated by this crazy rhythm of finishing things and smoking."

A businessman: "I smoked before I'd start a thing. Like dictating a letter or getting dressed in the morning. I guess I got into this sub-habit originally by telling myself I had to think over whatever it was I was about to start. But in the end this excuse didn't hold water. Does a man need to sit around and think before he gets dressed in the morning?"

A salesman: "One sub-habit I had was to smoke when

THE TOBACCO HABIT

I got into a taxicab. It was automatic: I'd fish in my pockets for a smoke while I was telling the guy where I wanted to go. The first time I got into a cab after I quit smoking, I suddenly felt completely disoriented. My hands went into my pockets for a cigarette and lighter that weren't there. I forgot where I wanted the cabby to take me. I must have sat there for about half a minute wondering where I wanted to go and what to do with my hands. That's how strong the habit had become."

A secretary: "I would always smoke when something upset me. It didn't have to be anything catastrophic. It could be—you know—any of the dozens of little problems that come up every day. I didn't really think about it, but I guess I felt the cigarette comforted me. If I'd thought about it I'd have realized that the cigarette only made me feel worse because I was always disgusted with myself for smoking too much. But I didn't think about it. It was pure habit."

. . .

Pure habit. A thing you do without a fully conscious decision. A sequence of motions that have been programed into your brain by years, perhaps decades, of repeated conditioning. Now do you understand more fully why it has been so hard to quit smoking in the past?

PART II

GATHERING THE FORCES

Now you're about to lay the foundation for your campaign to liberate yourself from tobacco. The stronger you make the foundation, the smoother your campaign will be.

4 🌲 *Why Do You Want to Quit?*

Sometime before you finish this chapter, get a piece of paper and pencil and begin listing all the reasons why you want to stop smoking, in order of their importance to you personally.

Keep this list handy over the next several days. Add to it. Change it. As you go through each day, smoking, ask yourself continually what you don't like about the habit. Even the smallest irritations should go on your list. Everything that bothers you to the slightest degree. Ashes on your desk. The smell of your fingers. Everything. The longer you make the list, the better.

The list will probably grow untidy as you add to it and shuffle the items' order of importance over the next few days. Go over it and over it until you're satisfied that it says what you personally think about smoking. Finally make a clean copy of it. It will be a permanent document that you will refer to often as your quit campaign progresses.

Your list won't be the same as other smokers'. It will be a personal document. Undoubtedly, it will contain some items that appear on almost everybody's list, but your order of importance won't be the same as the next man's or woman's. Quite possibly, too, your list will contain items that don't appear on another smoker's list: things that bother you but haven't particularly bothered him. And, conversely, he may have listed odd little irritations and hangups that have never disturbed you at all.

To help you get your thoughts organized, here's a checklist of items that we've heard smokers mention most often:

Major health fears. The United States government, and the governments of other nations around the world, have officially declared themselves to be against smoking because of its now-proven role in causing cancer, emphysema (a condition in which the lungs can't absorb oxygen efficiently), heart disease, and other serious or fatal conditions. There is no need to catalogue here all the research results that have led to these conclusions over the past decade, nor to reiterate all the frightening statistics on smokers' high incidence of disease and early death. You know the research results. You've read the statistics. If you're scared, good. You should be. But it is not the purpose of this book to terrify you into giving up cigarettes. We assume you picked up the book because you were already concerned about smoking, at least to some extent. Adding grossly to your fears would not serve our purpose or yours.

As a matter of fact, medical men have experimented with the idea of using health fears as a lever to pry people loose from cigarettes. It hasn't worked well.

Why Do You Want to Quit?

Smokers are adults, after all—at least most of them are. To sit them down and lecture them on the evils of tobacco, even though these evils are patently and demonstrably real, serves only to irritate most of them and make them angry. It doesn't actually help them stop smoking. It may make some of them increase their smoking because it increases their general nervousness.

So you will find no health lectures in this book. That isn't what we're here for. We aren't going to grab you by the lapels and shout, "You're killing yourself, you fool!" You're adult enough to develop this kind of concern all by yourself, with no help from us or anybody else.

But if major health worries are among your reasons for campaigning against smoking—and with most smokers, they are—put them on your list.

Current health problems. Few smokers feel they are as healthy right now as they'd like to be. Whether or not they worry seriously about cancer or heart disease or some other health catastrophe in the future, they are concerned or worried or maybe just annoyed by signs of failure that have already shown up in their bodies. For instance:

• Shortness of breath. You pant after walking up a few flights of stairs, maybe only one flight. You feel extremely tired after walking as little as a mile, especially a hilly mile. Recreations you once enjoyed—swimming, perhaps, or tennis or skiing—have become hard for you because you simply don't have the wind.

• Five o'clock slump. At the end of a long day's smoking, you feel a leaden weight of weariness each evening. You feel bleary-eyed, headachy, just generally unhealthy.

GATHERING THE FORCES

When other people are going out to seek the pleasures of the evening, you can only slump before a TV set, feeling like a puppet with cut strings.

- Morning head. You wake up headachy, not quite refreshed from the night's sleep. You feel as though your head is still exuding tobacco fumes.
- Cough and hoarseness. Your throat is sore, full of mucus. You have to clear your throat often as you talk. There's a constant, annoying tickle in your chest.
- Sore mouth. Your gums, tongue, palate, and lips are tender and perhaps afflicted with frequent sores or blisters. Your mouth stings when you brush your teeth or use mouthwash.

Cosmetic problems. Your teeth and fingers are yellowed. Your complexion is sallow because of the effects of smoking on blood circulation. There is some evidence, also, that smoking causes a prematurely-aged appearance by affecting the health of the skin and hastening lines and wrinkles.

Taste problems. Your mouth tastes bad in the mornings, especially after a night of drinking and smoking. Food doesn't taste as good to you as it once did.

Smell. Your clothes, hair, and skin smell of tobacco smoke. When you sit and smoke in a room, leave the room for a while, and then return, the stale tobacco odor annoys you. Your breath has a smoky odor. If this troubles you with your reduced sense of smell, you wonder how it seems to nonsmokers around you.

Why Do You Want to Quit?

Clutter and mess. Your home is cluttered with the debris of your habit: ashtrays full of butts, ashes strewn on floors and chairs, crumpled cigarette packs, half-used books of matches.

Sense of public nuisance. When you smoke in a public place, you're embarrassed by the knowledge that non-smokers around you are bothered by the smoke. Most are too polite to say so—a fact that makes you feel still worse.

Fire hazard. You remember occasions when you fell asleep holding a lighted cigarette, or left the house and forgot a cigarette burning in an ashtray. You were lucky then; you wonder if your luck will hold in the future. One Smoke Watchers' client told us of an occasion when he lit a cigarette in an airplane. He had one of those tricky lighters with a transparent fuel reservoir. In the reduced air pressure of the airplane cabin, some of the fuel had leaked out of the chamber and soaked his pocket and the entire surface of the lighter. When he started to light his cigarette, his hand was suddenly enveloped in flame. He had to go to a doctor for treatment of severe burns. "That bothered me, of course," he said, "but what bothered me worse was the thought of what could have happened if the newspaper I was reading or something else had caught on fire. Because of my smoking habit, I could have destroyed the airplane and killed dozens of innocent people." On that particular smoker's list of reasons for quitting, fire hazard was number one.

GATHERING THE FORCES

General nuisance effects. As a smoker, you're constantly bothered by the fact that you have only one free hand. If you have to pick up some bulky object or perform some other task that everybody else does easily and naturally with two hands, you must (1) try to do it with one hand and possibly fail ridiculously; or (2) try to do it with both hands while holding the cigarette, maybe burning your fingers; or (3) hold the cigarette in your mouth and get smoke in your eyes; or (4) put out the half-smoked cigarette and feel an irritating sense of loss. Cigarettes are always getting in your way.

Reduction of sexual potency or activity. Doctors don't know whether the cause lies in body chemistry or simply in the fact that smokers tire out at the end of the day, but the fact is that many smokers find their sex lives less interesting as they approach the age of forty. Those who stop smoking often report a startling, almost instantaneous revival of sexual drives.

Expense. If your cigarettes cost you 40¢ a pack and you smoke a pack a day, that adds up to nearly $150 a year. At two packs a day, you're spending almost $300 a year. Moreover, as a smoker you're likely to have generally poorer health than the average nonsmoker, so you pay extra during a typical year for doctors' and druggists' bills. You pay for a whole array of minor sicknesses that could be aggravated by your smoking habit: sore throats, sinusitis, headaches, mouth sores. You pay for other sicknesses that aren't directly caused by smok-

Why Do You Want to Quit?

ing but that prey on you because your body's general defenses are weak: diseases such as colds, flu, streptococcus infections. And in the end you may pay much more heavily—in money and in other ways—for serious illnesses such as cancer and heart disease.

Guilt over "setting a bad example." If there are children or teen-agers in your home, or if you spend any part of your time around youngsters who look up to you as an adult model to copy, you feel uncomfortable about your smoking. It's well known that youngsters are much more likely to become smokers if their parents smoke than if their parents don't. In one study at Princeton University, researchers gathered data on two groups of young men and women up to age thirty. In the nonsmoking group, it turned out, only twenty-four percent had come from homes in which one or both parents smoked. In the smoking group, sixty-seven percent had had at least one smoking parent; and another eleven percent recalled that, as children or teen-agers, they'd been close to some other admired adult—a teacher, an athletic coach, a camp counselor—who smoked.

General self-dissatisfaction. You're unhappy over the thought that tobacco has enslaved you. You're aware many other smokers have escaped the slavery; you're angry with yourself for being, as you imagine, too "weak" to gain your own freedom.

. . .

GATHERING THE FORCES

These are some of the more common items we've seen on smokers' lists. Now make your own list. Carry it around with you or keep it nearby as you go through your next few packs of cigarettes. Think hard about the habit and carefully notice every aspect of it that you don't like.

Don't show the list to a nonsmoker. To a smoker, yes; to an ex-smoker, fine. But not to a nonsmoker. He'll only laugh at you. "Well," he'll say, "if you hate smoking this much, why do you smoke?"

He won't be able to understand what you're going through. Only we smokers and ex-smokers can hope to understand. Only we can make any sense out of this magnificent paradox: to hate smoking, yet to smoke.

All right. Now read over your list. Have a cigarette. Observe your own reactions to the cigarette, your emotions, your thoughts about it.

Go ahead: *enjoy* it. Feel no guilt. You have taken the first steps toward becoming a nonsmoker. By the time you finish the course outlined in this book, you will enjoy *not* smoking as much as you are now enjoying that cigarette.

5 🌲 The Game of "Cold Turkey"

Knowing why you want to quit smoking is an important part of your psychological preparation. Another important part is knowing what method or methods you are going to use and why—and, as a corollary, why you are going to discard other possible methods.

It's important because you must have faith in the method you choose. Otherwise you may get halfway through your quit campaign and think, "This isn't working quite as fast as I'd hoped. Maybe some other method would be better. Maybe I should give up and start all over again." This is the downfall of many a smoker trying to stop.

So you've got to have faith. Enough to carry you all the way to the end of the line. Faith—but not blind faith. It must have a basis in reason, in a logical thinking-through of what's good and what isn't so good in your particular case.

. . .

Some smokers simply stop smoking. On Friday they smoke as much as they ever smoked, and they come home Friday night and say, "Never again," and on Saturday it turns out they mean it. On Saturday they do not smoke at all. Never again.

"Cold turkey," it's called. It has been pushed as the only possible way of quitting. "You can't cut down," they all tell you. "You can't taper off. The only way to quit is to quit, just plain quit. Cold turkey. Never touch a cigarette again."

Some very responsible and presumably authoritative people have made this statement, including the authors of some books similar to this one. Cold-turkey quitters themselves are likely to be loud boosters of the method. They're proud of themselves. Rightly so, of course. But they sometimes tend to let this pride inflate their egos a little. They look upon themselves as persons of iron will, unflinching self-control. They walk about the earth saying, "Look at me, look how strong I am!" And they urge the cold-turkey system upon everybody else, in much the same way as jogging enthusiasts and cold-baths-before-breakfast bugs and diet faddists urge their own particular systems of self-discipline upon other people. The act of preaching such self-discipline is actually, in many or most cases, simply a disguised form of bragging. The preacher says, in effect, "I am strong enough to do this thing this way. Are *you* strong enough? Are you afraid to try?"

Let the cold-turkey boosters preach and brag. Listen, nod politely, and go your way.

For we at Smoke Watchers are quite certain the cold-turkey system is not the only way or even necessarily

The Game of "Cold Turkey"

the best way. We know this to be true because we've proved it.

The system we've used so successfully and the one we'll explain to you in this book is not actually a system in the sense of having rigid, mechanical rules. It is more like—well, call it a philosophy. An approach. It is capable of endless variation to fit the needs and nature of each individual. You can incorporate other "systems" within it if you like, if you think they'll serve you well. Within the Smoke Watchers approach, you can go cold turkey. Or you can go warm chicken. Or you can go anywhere in between. Pick what seems right for you.

But we think you should be warned about some possible problems in the cold-turkey route. It's a tough way to go, and, understandably, many people have failed to make it and have then become needlessly discouraged.

For one thing, the cold-turkey route has a sometimes overwhelming tightrope quality. One misstep and you're finished. The two possible outcomes are total success or total failure; there's nowhere in between.

"I tried it seven different times," one smoker told us. He was a man of about forty-five who had been smoking since his early twenties. After using the Smoke Watchers approach he had been cigarette-free for more than a year and seemed perfectly confident that he would never smoke again, ever. He was now a confirmed nonsmoker. But he had previously lived through a lot of needless mental anguish in arriving at this happy state. We tape-recorded his account of his experiences because it illustrates so well what we think are some bad dangers in the cold-turkey idea:

"With the cold-turkey system, you see," he said, "you got too worried about yourself. The idea is that you quit all at once, you swear you'll never smoke another cigarette again. Okay. If you can get through the first week or two, I guess that's fine. Some people have done it. But I don't think everybody ought to expect that much of himself. Not everybody can hold out through those first bad days. And luck enters the picture too. If your life stays pretty tranquil the first few weeks, maybe you make it, you sail through and kick the habit. But maybe your luck doesn't hold. Something goes wrong, like you have a fight with your boss or somebody in your family gets sick. In my case, one time, I was doing all right—four days without a smoke—and then *crash!* A big life-insurance bill lands in my mailbox. It's a bill I've forgotten about. I mean, it comes every year at the same time but I've forgotten it's due. I'm not prepared for it. I have to do a lot of scrabbling around to get the money to pay it. And that's what brings me down. I have to have a cigarette, and then another, and—well, you know how it goes.

"Now, here's the point, you see. In the cold-turkey game, if you have one cigarette—*just one*—you've failed. I mean that's the psychology of it. The minute you light that first cigarette, you figure the whole deal is finished. You tell yourself, 'Well, it's no use, I can't make it. Here I am smoking again.' Just one cigarette kills the whole effort. There's no room in the deal for partial success or partial failure, no allowance for human frailty or mistakes. It's everything or nothing. Just because of some fluke of bad luck or some momentary lapse of willpower

The Game of "Cold Turkey"

or something, you instantly fail. That's what you're forced to believe. You tell yourself, 'Here I am smoking this cigarette. This means I'm a smoker again. So I might as well quit trying and go out and buy myself a carton of the damned things!' "

Thus did one ex-smoker portray the razor's-edge quality of the cold-turkey route. It appears to us to involve unnecessary risks for many or perhaps most smokers. If you're going to walk a tightrope, you can at least spread a net below you.

Another problem with the cold-turkey approach is that it represents an attempt to defeat a huge, multi-armed, enveloping enemy all at one blow.

Throughout this book we've been using the terms "tobacco habit" and "cigarette habit" and "smoking habit." In truth, however, what we are dealing with is not one habit but many. Your smoking complex is composed of dozens or even hundreds of small, interrelated habits tangled together into one enormous multi-habit.

The cigarette you smoke with your morning coffee is a small sub-habit all by itself. So are the cigarettes you smoke while driving your car. So are the cigarettes you light whenever you begin to dial a telephone. In addition, there are still smaller physical sub-habits: the little movements you make when reaching for a cigarette, lighting it, tapping it in an ashtray.

In later chapters we will consider these separate habits in detail. For now, we simply want to point out to you that these separate habits exist. Trying to overcome all of them simultaneously—the cold-turkey approach—seems almost ridiculously ambitious. To try this is to ask too much of yourself. This is why most cold-turkey campaigns fail.

It is far better, we believe, to attack the sub-habits one by one. Far easier, far more comfortable, far more sensible—and, as our records show, far more successful.

6 🌲 ...And Other Games

There are many other possible ways of quitting cigarettes, or cutting down your daily consumption, or kidding yourself into thinking you're doing so. Let's consider some of them briefly.

- *Pills.* There are several brands of stop-smoking pills and preparations on the market. They generally contain such substances as nicotine, lobeline, tranquilizers, aspirin, and other chemicals (see Chapter 3) in varying combinations.

They are honest products—the major brands, at any rate—and in most cases are honestly advertised. They do not and cannot claim to make you a nonsmoker automatically. If such a pill existed, there would obviously be no need for an organization such as Smoke Watchers nor for you to be reading this book. The stop-smoking pills typically advertise with phraseology like this:

"If you really *want* to stop smoking..."

"An aid for the smoker who is determined to break the cigarette habit . . . "

"We can't *make* you stop smoking. You must make the decision. But . . . "

And so on. The point is clear. Pills and other chemical preparations can be used in any quit campaign, but they're useful only if the campaign itself is effective. As the ads say, you've got to "want" and be "determined" and "make the decision" first, before you start swallowing the pills. The wanting and determining and deciding, of course, are the hard part.

Many Smoke Watchers' clients have taken pills while going through our course and have reported that they found the pills helpful. Fine. We say do whatever you think will help you. But we would utter a few words of caution. If you approach pills in the wrong way, they can do more harm than good.

The mistake some smokers make is to expect too much of pills. The result is a deep-down kind of discouragement that can last for years.

A thirty-two-year-old actress told us a typical story. She had become a very heavy smoker and was extremely worried about it, not only for health reasons but because cigarettes were making her voice hoarse—a distinct liability in her profession. She had tried to quit several times in her career but had failed. Determined to break the habit somehow, she sent away for some pills that were sold by mail order. The manufacturer's claims were rather extravagant, "but I believed what the ad said because I wanted to believe it. I thought the pills would be a substitute for my own willpower: I'd just take the pills and become a nonsmoker overnight."

It didn't work that way, of course. She took the pills

. . . And Other Games

faithfully for several days, waiting for the magical disappearance of her wish to smoke. But the wish remained, irresistible as always. On the fourth day she was smoking just as heavily as she had ever smoked. And—worse yet—she now had the feeling she was tobacco's slave for life.

"I felt I'd tried everything there was to be tried," she told us. "I felt that if not even pills could help me quit smoking, nothing ever could."

She was then twenty-nine years old. For the next three years she continued to smoke heavily, resigned to the belief that she was a confirmed and incurable smoker. This was the damage done by a mistaken approach to anti-tobacco pills.

- *Dummy cigarettes.* These are cigarette-shaped tubes of paper or plastic, sometimes with menthol or some other flavoring substance in the middle. You don't light them; you merely hold them in your mouth or between your fingers as you would a cigarette. The theory is that this gives you, harmlessly, some of the same satisfactions you might get from real cigarettes: something to put in your mouth, something to hold in your hand.

Dummy cigarettes are, indeed, harmless. But most smokers report little else in their favor. Two British researchers, Dr. Keith P. Ball and Dr. Miller Mair, studied various tobacco-withdrawal ideas in a large-scale program in London from 1962 to 1966, and they concluded: "Dummy cigarettes were not considered of much help." Nor were pills. Placebos (plain sugar pills that the smokers believed to contain some kind of medication) "appeared equally effective."

GATHERING THE FORCES

If you believe dummy cigarettes can help or comfort you, by all means use them as you go through your Smoke Watchers course. But expect no magical results from them.

- *Cigarette holders and filters.* These are essentially a means of kidding oneself. Many smokers, afraid or otherwise unwilling to attack the cigarette habit directly, have taken to using cigarette holders (some of which advertise amazing effectiveness in trapping smoke tars and nicotine) or have switched to filter-tipped cigarette brands that make similar claims. In this way, the deluded smoker believes, he is cutting down his intake of harmful smoke ingredients without actually cutting down his smoking.

Is he? Perhaps to a very small extent. But nobody yet knows for certain precisely what smoke ingredients cause what human ailments, nor what quantities of any ingredient are necessary to cause any given disease. A filter that traps X percent of tars and nicotine may actually be doing no good at all. It may still let through enough tars and nicotine to do damage—or the tars and nicotine may not in fact be the main causes of the damage. The causes may lie in some yet-unsuspected smoke ingredient that gets through the filter unimpeded.

For reasons that we'll make clear when the time comes, we will counsel you to change cigarette brands for a brief period as you go through the Smoke Watchers course. This may involve switching from an unfiltered to a filter-tip brand. But don't delude yourself that this act alone represents a significant cutting-down or will by itself improve your health or lengthen your life expect-

... *And Other Games*

ancy. Our reasons for counseling a brand switch are not based on any faith in filter tips or filtering holders. All smokers are smokers, no matter by what route the smoke reaches their lungs.

Science has not yet come up with a demonstrably effective way of attacking cigarette smoke and rendering it harmless to all smokers. But there is an excellent way of making it harmless to you personally. You do it by attacking your smoking habit.

7 🙡 *Not Stopping but Starting*

You are now almost ready to launch yourself into your quit campaign. But there is one enormously important shift of mental attitude that you must accomplish first. In a way it is a psychological trick that you must play on yourself.

You must look upon your quit campaign not as the end of something pleasant, but as *the beginning of something even better.*

Get out your list of reasons for quitting (Chapter 4). Study it. Think of the pleasures of being without your tobacco habit. Think how it will feel to be free.

Don't think of what you are about to do as a kind of martyrdom, a self-sacrifice, a giving-up of something you enjoyed. In a sense, of course, it is. We can't kid you and you can't kid yourself about that. But you're an adult. You can look ahead as well as back. The man or woman you are about to become—the nonsmoker—will be by all standards healthier and happier than what you are now. Prouder, too. You won't be a slave any longer. You will be free and you will have earned your freedom through your own effort. You will *like* yourself better.

Not Stopping but Starting

We are aware this all has a faintly corny sound. Some of our more sophisticated clients have occasionally laughed at us for saying it. No matter. It must be said. You must go into your quit campaign with a positive, not negative, attitude. If you don't, your chances of success are not good.

"Quit" is a bad word in this sense. You are not quitting so much as starting: entering a new life, probably a longer life, certainly a better life. Fix this in your mind and never let it come loose: *I am making a new me.* From this point on, don't ever use the words "quit" or "stop" or phrases like "break away from." Think instead of the happiness you are about to win for yourself. You are about to be reborn.

The word "quit" is sprinkled through the chapters that have preceded this one. We had to use the word so you would know what we were talking about. It is the common word for the process we are considering. It is universally used and understood among smokers. "I'm going to quit," they tell each other. "I wish I could quit." "I really ought to quit." All right. We adopted the common word and stuck with it while introducing our subject. From now on, however, we will use the word but rarely. It is a negative word with all the wrong connotations. From now on, we will substitute other words and phrases. "Coming free" is one possible phrase. A word that we like even better is "succeeding."

When we Americans say someone has succeeded—when we say, "he's a success"—we imply many things. We imply that we envy him. We imply that he has defeated some adversary or risen to the top of some world of endeavor. We mean he is rich in some way: in money, in sexual enjoyment, in general contentment.

A former smoker who becomes a true nonsmoker is a success in all these senses. He is envied; he has overcome; he has risen; he is rich. For these reasons, the words "succeed" and "success" will be used often in this book from now on.

If you don't like our words, use your own. Whatever your word or phrase is, it should not be anything like "quit" or "stop." It should not embody any thought of leaving something behind. It should have no sadness in it, no regret, no sense of pain or sacrifice. Make it a forward-looking phrase. Make it magnificent. Make it corny: who cares? We are not in the business of producing great literature here. We are in the business of coming free from tobacco: saving health, saving life. If a little corn can help accomplish that, we are perfectly willing to live with it. The price seems ridiculously small when compared with what we're buying.

We've heard all kinds of corny and glorious phrases from our clients over the years. One woman referred to what she was doing as the "Unyellowing Process." She intended the phrase as a double-entendre. She meant, first, that she no longer hated herself as a coward; she no longer submitted meekly to the domination of cigarettes; she had stood up straight and asserted herself and grown tall in her own estimation. The word "unyellowing" also referred to her physical coloring. "I hated the way cigarettes made my fingers yellow," she told us. "And when I was smoking I always used to feel I was turning yellow all over. You know: my teeth, the whites of my eyes. That was the feeling I got. Now I feel I'm the color I ought to be." There was, indeed, a physical basis for her feeling. Smoking interferes with blood circulation and, in white persons, can produce a marked

Not Stopping but Starting

sallowness of complexion. As these people come free from tobacco, there is often a startlingly quick change in skin tone. Their cheeks become rosier in a matter of days; their entire complexion abruptly takes on a fresher, healthier look.

A businessman who succeeded at the age of sixty-three, after more than forty years of smoking, liked to use a word drawn from his management experience: "Reorganization." He explained: "A company reorganizes when it sees its old setup isn't serving it well any more: competitors are passing it by, it's losing markets, it's on the downgrade. So it puts itself through a radical change, maybe even an upheaval. It lops off all the musty old departments that weren't making money any more, busts up the hierarchy of tradition-bound old men who were holding it back, makes itself tough and lean again. That's the kind of thing I feel I'm doing now. I'm making myself younger and stronger. Tougher. A better competitor."

"This whole thing has some crazy sexual overtones for me," a younger man told us. "I call it 'Sexing Up.' It's funny how it came about. When I first made up my mind to go through with this, I knew I was going to need something to occupy my thoughts—you know, keep me from brooding about cigarettes. I knew this was one of the things you had to do because I'd talked to other nonsmokers. For a long time, before I actually took the plunge, I worried about this. I didn't know quite what I was going to use to keep me from brooding. Well, one night when I was going home from a girl's apartment, an amazing thought hit me. At least, it seemed amazing. I was still a smoker then, and I was burning up easily two packs a day. That's at least one cigarette every half-hour.

But while I'd been with this girl I hadn't smoked at all for over two hours. Hadn't even thought about a cigarette. I mean, you can't smoke when you're—well, that's how it started. I thought, 'Nothing can take a man's mind off smoking better than sex.' So when I took the plunge and joined your course, I deliberately became a kind of swinger. I surrounded myself with girls. And the beautiful part of it was, I found I was actually sexier without cigarettes. I wasn't tired at night, I was jumping with nervous energy. I wasn't embarrassed about tobacco breath. It was great. And whenever I started to think about cigarettes and feel sorry for myself, I switched onto this positive idea. I told myself, 'You're not losing cigarettes, man, you're gaining sex. Sexing Up.'"

To each his own route. The point is, you must fix in your mind a strong awareness of everything you are about to win, rather than the one unimportant thing you are about to lose. You are going to be a success.

PART III

THE TECHNIQUES OF SUCCESS

Here are the weapons you will use directly against your own cigarette complex. Like any weapons, they are effective only when used well. Be sure you understand them thoroughly before finally picking them up and committing yourself to the attack.

8 ❦ *The Benevolent Pressure Group*

If the philosophy of Smoke Watchers could be said to have a cornerstone, a single major idea of supreme importance, it would be this:

Since social pressures made you start smoking, you must use social pressures to help you succeed.

Like thousands of other smokers, Fred J. (Chapter 3) tried to wrestle with his smoking habit all by himself. He went to a cabin in the woods and tried to succeed alone. Like the majority of others who have gone this route, he failed.

True, there are large numbers of ex-smokers who have pulled off the trick by themselves. But they are distinctly in the minority. No precise statistics are available, of course, on the actual numbers of smokers who have tried to come free, nor on how many have succeeded after how many attempts, nor on how many have failed. Smoke Watchers' own statistics, based on the case histories of clients, indicate that fewer than fifteen percent of all individual attempts to break the tobacco habit— that is, attempts by lone individuals—actually succeed.

THE TECHNIQUES OF SUCCESS

A discouraging record indeed. And an indication of the habit's strength.

No: you cannot reasonably hope to succeed by yourself. You can hope, but it isn't a reasonable hope. The chances against you are too high. The odds are so unfavorable that few horse players or Wall Street speculators would like to put money on you. Perhaps you have already learned this fact through personal experience: you've tried to come free alone at least once, maybe many times, and each time have enjoyed a fitful and restless freedom for a few days and finally have collapsed in defeat.

All right. Don't try it again. Instead of struggling your painful way along the route by yourself, you are going to saunter down it in company

We aren't here to kid you. We don't say it will be a lark. We do say you'll find it quite comfortable. You're going to be surprised.

. . .

Your first step is to associate with a benevolent pressure group of other smokers who are trying to come free, as you are.

Think back, if you can, and reconstruct the social pressures that swirled around you on the day you smoked your first cigarette—and in the months that followed as you gradually increased your cigarette consumption and finally became habituated. Recall how it was, how it felt.

Were you trying to impress people with your adulthood? Your sophistication, your toughness, your urbanity? Were you trying to impress a particular member of the opposite sex, or the opposite sex in general? Were

The Benevolent Pressure Group

you trying to look or seem sexier, amorously adventurous? Were you, at the same time, trying to impress those of your own sex—increase your stature among them, win applause for your worldly wisdom? Were you trying to look and feel like a "thinking" man or woman? Did a cigarette help you take yourself seriously?

Your memory may contain bits and pieces of all these elements and perhaps others. Sort them out. Ponder them. The important point is that these were all pressures exerted upon you by other people—subtly and unintentionally, but powerfully. You reacted to the pressures because you, like all the rest of us, were a member of society with a need to get along in it and succeed within it. You may have been alone when you smoked your first cigarette, you may even have smoked alone in front of mirrors for many months in the beginning, but you were still smoking because of social pressures. There was no individual biological mechanism inside you that forced you to do what you were doing. Your body did not need the smoke. Your psyche didn't need the smoke either, but it seemed at the time to need the *act* of smoking. The act of lighting, holding, and drawing on a cigarette seemed to fill some gap or prove some point or serve some other vaguely recognized need in your life at the time.

It was silly, but it happened. It happened to millions of us.

Very well. You can now make the same process work for you in your bid for success. The subtle but extremely powerful pressures exerted by other people are going to make you *want not to smoke*.

. . .

THE TECHNIQUES OF SUCCESS

There are many possible ways of associating yourself with, or gathering around you, a group of smokers who want to succeed. Obviously the easiest way is to join a group already in existence.

It is likely, for instance, that one or more Smoke Watchers groups are operating somewhere in your vicinity. Each such group has been formed by and is led by a professional counselor, himself or herself an ex-smoker, carefully trained by us in the principles outlined in this book.

If it isn't practical for you to join a regular Smoke Watchers group, you can seek groups of other kinds. Many anti-tobacco groups are being operated by various public and private agencies all over the country: hospitals, regional and local offices of health organizations such as the American Cancer Society, fraternal organizations, municipal government agencies, schools and colleges. You may want to join such a group if one is handy.

The group you find may not operate on the basis this book outlines. Its attractive characteristic will be that it *is* a group. If you join it, listen carefully to what its leader or counselor says, but continue to study this book and apply its principles within the framework of the group effort. Smoke Watchers has proven that these principles are sound and workable. We honestly know of no better way to success.

If you can't find or don't want to join an existing group, simply seek out other smokers who are trying to defeat smoking as you are. Deliberately associate with these people. From the beginning, tell them about your plans for coming free and listen to their plans. As often as possible, from then on, tell them about your progress

The Benevolent Pressure Group

and ask about theirs. Stay in touch with them throughout your entire campaign

They need not be close friends. They can be simply people you meet once in a while on a commuter train or at a supermarket. As a matter of fact, we've found at Smoke Watchers that the best kind of anti-smoking group doesn't consist entirely of close friends and emphatically not of relatives. (The reasons will become apparent later.) Thus, don't attempt to round up a family group. And unless it comes about naturally, don't attempt to gather a group of close friends and pressure them all into joining in your campaign.

You should meet at least once a week if possible. You don't have to hold formal meetings. Just be sure that these are people whom you'll run into at frequent intervals.

They can be people in your car pool, bowlers in your league, or simply people you see occasionally in some social setting. This is fine. Of course, keep the group small, since a larger group requires professional management. The only other possible difficulty is that there may be an unwanted degree of homogeneity and closeness in the group. The best group is a heterogeneous group, made up of both sexes, all income brackets, all walks of life. The idea will be to concentrate attention on the one problem you all have in common: your habituation to cigarettes. If there are other, extraneous emotional associations among members of the group, you won't be able to help each other so effectively.

Don't try to bulldoze people into joining your campaign. Almost all smokers have some degree of self-consciousness about the habit, and some will react with self-defensive anger to any suggestion that they should not smoke. Occasionally, at Smoke Watchers meetings, a member turns up who is not there entirely of his own free will. He has been badgered into attending by his spouse or a doctor or a group of friends. He may attend simply to get the others off his back, with no intention of taking the program seriously. Or he may come with a half-formed wish to succeed but without much faith in his capacity to do so. Either way, such a member in a small group is not likely to be successful and might be disruptive. He is angry, irritable, unhappy. He looks at the program in the wrong way. To him it's "quitting," not "coming free" or "succeeding." His only real chance for success is with a professionally run group.

So don't go up to a friend, stare him in the eye, and say, "I see you're a smoker. You ought to quit, you know. You're ruining your health. . . ." He will tell you (quite properly) to go away and mind your own business.

Handle it more gently. Tell him about your own tobacco problems: "I've been wanting to quit smoking for years. . . . " (You'll have to use the word "quit" because it's the universally understood word.) "I've tried several times but it never worked. Now I'm thinking of trying a new approach, a program developed by Smoke Watchers. . . . "

At this point you aren't asking him to join anything or do anything; nor are you challenging his tobacco habit. You can both smoke comfortably as you talk. If he's interested, explain more about the program. If he's still interested, lend him a copy of this book or send him to the library for one. Stay in touch with him.

. . .

The Benevolent Pressure Group

All right, now you're associated with other smokers who all want to come free. What do they do? What happens to them?

Later we'll show you the mechanics of the process in detail. For the moment, let's just look at the psychodynamics of the group. What are these "benevolent pressures" and how do they work?

At a typical Smoke Watchers meeting, each new member—or every member if this is a newly formed group—tells who he is, what his experience with tobacco has been, how long he has been a smoker, and how much he now smokes. This is done informally. The member doesn't stand up and give an address; he simply sits and talks casually. Other members can make comments or ask him questions if they like.

Toward the end of the meeting, each member announces his plans for the coming week: whether to maintain his present level of smoking or (preferably, of course) cut down. To avoid confusion, all references to "level" or "amount" of smoking are specifically in terms of *the number of cigarettes smoked per day.*

In succeeding meetings, each member tells how he has fared in the preceding week. Did he cut down his smoking by the amount he planned last week? How did he find the experience? Hard? Easy? If he hasn't achieved what he planned, what does he think the reasons have been? Other members are invited to comment on what he says. What do *they* think his trouble has been? What are their suggestions for improving his performance next week? What experiences have they (particularly the longer-term members) had in their own campaigns that might be relevant or helpful?

As the meetings progress, each member finds himself

THE TECHNIQUES OF SUCCESS

being pushed gently but ever more insistently by the group's will. A psychosocial situation develops in which each man and woman seeks to win the group's approval and applause. Just as the need for group approval forced each to start smoking years ago, the same social pressure now acts in the opposite direction. Sometimes slowly but usually quite steadily, each smoker is pushed toward his success. He finds that he *must* keep moving toward it if he is to maintain his social standing in the group; he is uncomfortable if he doesn't.

To see the process at work, consider this transcript from a typical Smoke Watchers meeting:

Counselor (to a member): "Well, Joe, how about you? Last week you were down to—let's see (consults Joe's record card)—nineteen cigarettes a day. You said you were going to cut out four this week, you were going down to fifteen. How did you do?"

Joe (proudly): "Made it. No problem."

A woman member who was still up in the thirty-a-day range: "That's great! Which four did you cut out?"

Joe: "Well, I tackled my sub-habit of smoking while driving a car. On a regular workday I was smoking four of these cigarettes, two going to work in the mornings and two coming back at night."

Woman: "You killed the whole sub-habit?"

Joe: "All of it. I didn't want those driver's cigarettes much anyway. They were mostly 2's." (He refers to Smoke Watchers' system of rating each cigarette according to how much you want it, from *5*, meaning very much, to *1*, meaning very little. This system will be explained in detail in a later chapter.)

Another member, a university graduate student who

The Benevolent Pressure Group

had worked his way down from over sixty cigarettes to zero and hoped soon to leave the group, completely free: "So what are you going to do next week?"

Joe (shifts uncomfortably in his chair): "Well, I figured I'd stay at the fifteen-a-day level for one more week. You know: kind of get used to it."

Graduate student: "Seems silly to stop now, Joe. You were smoking about fifty when you joined, weren't you? And you've come down steadily the whole time since then. Why stop? I mean, why lose your momentum?"

Woman: "That makes sense. Why don't you cut out some minor sub-habit? I mean an easy one."

Joe: "Well, I—"

Another woman member: "I used to have a sub-habit of smoking while I was waiting for a bus. I didn't want those cigarettes as much as I originally thought I did. I didn't miss them much when they were gone."

Graduate student: "Matter of fact, you don't miss any cigarettes that much."

Joe (with grumpy good humor): "What are you doing, bragging?"

Graduate student: "No, I'm just telling it like it is."

Counselor: "Why don't you tackle some minor sub-habit next? Seems to me I remember you mentioning one last week. What was it?"

Joe: "I guess I was talking about my newspaper cigarettes. I usually smoke one while I'm reading the morning paper and one with the evening paper."

First woman: "That's only a two-cigarette habit. You could kill it easily."

Joe: "Maybe I could break it into two sections. Kill the morning-paper cigarette this week and the evening one next week."

Graduate student: "Seems like a pretty slow way to go about it. You don't have to go that slow."

Joe: "But the trouble is—see, the evening-paper cigarette is one I want a lot. I usually rate it, like, 4. I figured I'd want to save it and tackle it at some later stage. You have to go at your own pace, right?"

Graduate student: "But it sounds like you want to slow down to a crawl. You'll lose all your momentum."

Counselor: "Why don't you just try it, Joe? Tackle those two newspaper cigarettes. We won't shoot you if you don't make it."

Joe (after a pause): "All right. Put me down for thirteen cigarettes a day next week. I'll come down to thirteen."

Graduate student: "Go-go, Joe!"

Thus did the group's benevolent social pressures keep one typical member on the track. (Parenthetical note: the main protagonist in this little drama, Joe, pushed on to complete success. Our records show that he did in fact drop down to thirteen cigarettes a day in the week following this meeting, to ten the following week, then to four, and finally to zero. That was six months ago. As far as we know, he has remained a nonsmoker since.)

Without the social pressures behind him, Joe in all probability would have suffered the fate of most smokers who try to succeed alone. If he had managed to work his way down to fifteen cigarettes a day (which is itself unlikely), he would probably have stopped there, as he wanted to when this meeting took place. He would have rationalized with himself in the manner familiar to all

The Benevolent Pressure Group

smokers. "I'll just stay at this level for a while," he'd have told himself. "Just for a while."

Possibly he would, indeed, have moved off the fifteen-a-day level after "just a while." But he would have moved upward, back toward his original level of fifty a day. Joe would not have come free alone.

He needed other people. So do you.

As we've said, it isn't necessary for you to organize a formal group, write a set of bylaws, and set up a schedule of regular weekly meetings. What you're seeking, essentially, is benevolent social pressure. You can find this informally in much the same way as it's found through the more formalized setup of a Smoke Watchers group. The main point is to associate with other smokers who are trying to win and talk with them from time to time—the more often and regularly, the better. Each time you meet, tell them your past week's progress and outline your goals for the coming week or so. Deliberately put yourself in the position of trying to earn their applause and feeling faintly ashamed when you don't.

Without at least some form of social pressure, your chances of breaking the tobacco habit are quite slim.

9 ⸙ The "Partner" System

A benevolent pressure group gets together once a week or so. Is that enough?

For some smokers, apparently, yes. Earlier in the history of Smoke Watchers, the once-a-week meeting was the only contact our smokers had with each other; and this seemed to provide enough social pressure and support for slightly fewer than two-thirds of them. The other third, however, ran into difficulties. If a meeting was scheduled on a Wednesday, they might do well on Thursday and Friday but begin to slip on Saturday. By Saturday, the group seemed too far away, the pressures too distant, too weak.

"Weekends are always my toughest times," one typical member, a suburban housewife, told us. "That's when you've got parties and drinking and everything. It's hard to stick to my goal on Saturday night. Like, last week I said I was going to drop down from ten cigarettes a day to seven, and I did it with no trouble Thursday and Friday. But on Saturday I smoked more. I don't know how many more, I lost count. I kept wishing there would

The "Partner" System

be a meeting on Saturday or Sunday. Once a week doesn't seem to be enough for me."

What she said—and many others echoed it—made excellent sense. Social pressure seems to be something like gravitation: its strength fades rapidly with distance. During the week, between meetings, all group members are out in the world where social pressures work in the wrong direction, urging people to smoke.

But to schedule more than one meeting a week would be too burdensome for most members. Most smokers are somewhat gregarious and have other activities of various kinds to attend to. So what could be done?

After pondering the matter for a long time, we developed what we call the "partner" system. Each group member is voluntarily paired with another; the two are partners or buddies—or whatever term they want to use. (If the group consists of an odd number of people, a triangular arrangement of three partners is just as workable.) The partners set up some mutually-convenient time for talking to each other, usually by phone, regularly once a day Each tells the other his problems of the day, checks on the other's progress. The two help maintain each other's optimism and represent a continuation of the group's benevolent pressures throughout the week.

Partners should also be prepared to receive each other's calls when emergencies arise at other times of the day. This system has been used for many years by such organizations as Alcoholics Anonymous, and it works exceedingly well. When a former alcoholic feels a pressing need to have a drink, he phones another member. Often, merely the sound of a friendly and understanding voice on the phone is enough to get him through the emergency period. At other times, the called member may feel it necessary to rush to the caller's home and be with him in person as he struggles against the urge to drink. With smokers—who, unlike alcoholics, are not battling a hard physical addiction—the emergency is never that serious. A simple phone conversation is almost always enough.

One businessman, for instance, had an arrangement with his partner (a schoolteacher) to talk by phone every morning at 8:30. But once in a while the businessman would also phone his fellow smoker at night. "I'd phone him before I went out to a cocktail party or dinner party," the businessman told us. "I really needed to hear his voice then. I knew I was going to want cigarettes when I started drinking that first cocktail. He'd agree how hard it was and tell me about his own troubles at parties. He'd remind me not to take any cigarettes with me, so if I wanted one I'd have to bum one. We'd laugh and joke a lot. It was a great help. All through the party, when I wanted a cigarette, I kept thinking how much I'd fall in this man's estimation if I had to phone him next morning and say I'd gone over my smoking limit. I kept hearing his voice telling me he knew it was hard, but not that hard. Later on, when I was finally down to zero cigarettes, I found that the ones I didn't have at parties were the ones I didn't really miss at all."

. . .

Who should your partner be? He or she can be virtually anyone, *but should not be a relative.*

Spouses and other relatives have too many intricately

The "Partner" System

tangled emotional ties among them. Casual acquaintances, especially those who move in different social circles, can discuss social problems and pressures frankly without much embarrassment, but members of the same family—and sometimes close friends—may find it difficult. Moreover, another danger in having a relative as your partner is that any family crisis, even a minor one, can upset what should be essentially a calm relationship between you.

In Smoke Watchers groups, partners are usually assigned to each other in random fashion by the counselor. If you pick your own partner, however, pick someone other than your closest friend. It's generally best to pick someone of your own sex, to avoid possible difficulties in discussing personal problems that relate to smoking. However, this isn't an absolutely essential requirement. The main point is that your partner should be someone with whom you can talk comfortably, preferably a casual acquaintance.

Having picked or been assigned your partner, your next step is to set up a daily telephone contact—some time of day when both of you can get to a phone easily and neither will be too rushed to talk leisurely. The phone conversations should include the following elements:

• Each of you should know the other's smoking level and the quota he has set for himself that week. Check up on each other daily.

• Each should tell the other about any particular problems that have come up in relation to smoking, especially if one of you has exceeded his self-imposed limit that day.

• Once in a while, review each other's reasons for

THE TECHNIQUES OF SUCCESS

wanting to be a nonsmoker (Chapter 4). You'll find this will help reinforce your positive attitude toward your campaign—the idea that you aren't "quitting" but are moving toward a new and better life.

So much for the daily phone contacts. Be sure to provide for emergency contacts as well. Sometimes this can be done in advance. If you know or sense that some period of tension is about to come up in your life, some situation in which the temptation to smoke will be stronger than normal, arrange to phone your partner before or during the period. Such a situation might be anything from a family crisis to a Saturday-night party.

In case of an unexpected emergency, you and your partner should also stand ready to listen to each other. Obviously you can't both hang around your telephones all day just in case the other wants to call. But each should let the other know about his general schedule, giving phone numbers where he can most likely be reached at various times of the day and week.

You and your partner should also meet face-to-face about once a week. If you can't find other Smoke Watchers to meet with, then the two of you should meet alone. As we've said, any kind of benevolent social pressure—even if it exists between only two people—is better than none at all.

10 ❦ The Problem of Countervailing Pressure

Just as it's important for you to be pushed forward and supported by a benevolent pressure group, it's essential that—at the same time—you avoid countervailing pressures, pressures in the opposite and wrong direction.

Essentially, these countervailing pressures come from the same broad environment of forces that pushed you into being a smoker in the first place. The general social environment in which you live, the environment *outside your benevolent pressure group*, wants you to smoke and will conspire against your efforts to succeed. What you must do, therefore, is shut that environment off to as great an extent as possible.

Your major problems are likely to come from your family and close friends, whether or not they are smokers.

If they are smokers, they will try to belittle your effort to succeed. We've pointed out before that success breeds envy, and envy is what you'll be battling. Other smokers will attempt to protect their own egos by pretending that what you're doing is unimportant and silly. You've heard their typical self-defensive statements dozens of times. In fact, possibly you've used such statements yourself in the past:

"When a doctor tells me to stop smoking, I'll stop...."

"Cancer, shmancer. Statistically, I could get killed easier driving a car than smoking...."

"When your time comes, you go—whether you're a smoker or not...."

"My grandfather smoked two packs a day till he was ninety-three...."

"Friend of mine never smoked in his life, keeled over from a heart attack when he was forty-one...."

This is what you'll hear, again and again, if you don't protect yourself in advance. Other smokers don't want you to succeed.

If they are nonsmokers, you'll get a different form of static. They simply won't understand what you're trying to do or what you're going through. They will tend to ridicule your efforts. "If you don't want to smoke, why don't you simply stop?" they'll ask. They may also come at you with a certain attitude of self-righteousness. They won't say it in so many words, but they will try to convey the notion that they are much more sensible than you are. "See how foolish you are," their attitude will say. "Why weren't you as smart as *we* were back then, when you started to smoke? Why couldn't you look into the future, as *we* did, and see the trouble you've got

The Problem of Countervailing Pressure

yourself into now? Look at you! Maybe you'll listen to us wiser voices from now on."

You may also hear similar nonsense from ex-smokers, particularly those few who have gone cold turkey and succeeded. Many ex-smokers are highly sympathetic to others embarking on an anti-cigarette campaign; they remember what it was like; they sincerely want to help even if only by standing out of the way. But others, especially cold-turkey types, will tend to blow their horns rather loudly. "You don't need all that pressure-group business," they will crow. "Look at me. I simply quit." What they mean to suggest, of course, is that they are stronger than you are.

All these pressures will be brought to bear against you within your family and your circle of friends. To forestall the pressures as effectively as possible, we suggest that you:

(1) Don't tell everybody in sight that you are on an anti-cigarette campaign. There is no need to keep it a secret, but there is no need to broadcast it either. Tell only those who would find out anyway. This will limit the number of people who could exert countervailing pressures against you.

(2) Ask your family members, friends, and work colleagues to leave you alone. To help you do this, we've written a sample letter to those people who might damage your campaign. The letter appears on page 82. As circumstances dictate, you can cut the letter out of the book and show it to people, or pin it to a family bulletin board, or retype it and distribute it, or simply paraphrase the gist of it as you talk to people. However you choose to go about it, some such message should be put

THE TECHNIQUES OF SUCCESS

A LETTER FROM A SMOKER

Dear Family Members and Friends:

I am about to embark on a campaign to free myself from the cigarette habit. The campaign is important to me, though I realize it may not seem so to you. My success or failure will depend in large part on the cooperation I get from those around me.

To put it simply, directly, and perhaps bluntly, I need only one thing from you: to be left alone.

This may seem to you like a somewhat rude request, but I don't intend it as such. The experience of other smokers who have gone this route before me—both those who have succeeded and those who haven't—shows that even the best-intentioned advice and comment from others can do damage to such a campaign.

Think back, if you can, to the last time you were in some difficult or trying situation and other people were commenting and counseling from the sidelines. Do you remember how it was? Somebody may have made a comment that he thought was funny, but it certainly wasn't funny to you. Somebody else may have offered what he thought was a piece of sound advice, but to you this advice was only an added irritation or an extra element of confusion. Almost everything said by bystanders, even when it was said with goodwill, simply made another pothole in the already rough road you had to travel.

This is why I ask you to leave me alone with my campaign. Ignore it as best you can. Please say nothing to me about it.

I'll be grateful for your understanding.

                     Sincerely,

                     ....

The Problem of Countervailing Pressure

across to everybody with whom you are in regular contact and who could conceivably exert countervailing pressures against you.

This message should keep most people from becoming nuisances during your climb to success. However, there may still be some who fail to understand the message, and you may have fleeting contacts with other people to whom you've never given the message: strangers on trains and planes, for example, who see you using your cigarette rating form (Chapter 11) and become curious and end by giving you unsolicited advice. It's important that you be prepared in advance to handle such situations. As we've said before, the campaign you are about to launch is a delicately balanced psychological one that can be influenced by seemingly minor events. A word of ridicule or a piece of ill-considered advice, even from a stranger, can weaken your resolve at a critical time or turn you from your successful path onto some odd sidetrack that leads nowhere.

How do you handle this kind of situation? The best advice we can give you is to cut such episodes short whenever possible. Above all, never get into an argument about the "best" way to succeed. If somebody starts telling you he knows a better way than yours, cool him fast by nodding politely and saying, "Yes, of course, everybody has his own methods. What's best for you wouldn't necessarily be best for me. . . . " If your friend continues to talk about his pet theory, repeat your statement in different words. Nothing stops an argument faster than simply refusing to debate.

Your friend's "best" method may, indeed, be an excellent one. It may have helped him and others succeed against cigarettes, just as he so ardently claims. But that isn't the point. The point is that you have embarked on a certain course; you want to see it through to its successful end. There is no future in letting other people continually switch you onto other courses. That way, obviously, you will never get to the end of anything.

11 🌲 *The Rating Form*

Now you're associated with other smokers who can exert benevolent social pressure on you, you're paired with a partner, and you're prepared against countervailing pressures. What next?

The next step is to begin using something that we call the "cigarette-rating form." This form will have various uses at various stages of your progress. We will explain these uses at the appropriate times. You must maintain this rating form throughout your campaign.

Essentially, the rating form is a means of analyzing the various sub-habits that, added together, make up your smoking complex. On this form, each day, you enter certain items of data about *every cigarette you smoke*.

Turn to the following page and glance at the sample rating form for a moment.

This is only a sample form. You can make your own rough copies of it easily enough by using any lined notebook. You will need one form per day—one or two notebook pages, depending on how many cigarettes you

THE TECHNIQUES OF SUCCESS

Day _____

	TIME	ACTIVITY	DESIRE	AMOUNT SMOKED
1				
2				
3				
4				
5				
6				
7				
8				
9				
10				
11				
12				
13				
14				
15				
16				
17				
18				
19				
20				

smoke per day. As you reduce your smoking, of course, your forms will grow shorter.

On the top of each form or page, put the day of the week and the date. Below that, you make a complete record of one day's smoking.

Notice that the form is made up of horizontal bars, divided into three boxes or sections apiece. Each of these bars refers to one cigarette, numbered in sequence

The Rating Form

through the day. The bar numbered "1" refers to the first cigarette you smoke in the morning, and so on.

In the left-hand section of each bar, you put down the time of day at which you smoked this cigarette.

In the middle section, you enter the activity you were engaged in at the time—drinking coffee, talking on the phone, driving to work, and so on.

In the right-hand box or section of each bar, you write any number from 1 to 5, indicating how much you wanted that particular cigarette. Use this rating scale:

1. No real desire.
2. Very little.
3. Moderate.
4. Very much.
5. Desperate need.

In other words, the more you want a cigarette, the higher you score it on this scale.

To the right of each bar is a schematic drawing of a cigarette. On this schematic drawing you indicate how much of this particular cigarette you smoked before putting it out. Do this by shading or otherwise marking off the smoked portion, starting at the right. (In other words, imagine that the lighted end of the cigarette is pointing to the right.) If you smoked only one-third of the cigarette, shade or otherwise mark the right-hand third of the schematic drawing. If you smoked it all the way down to the butt, shade or mark off the entire drawing.

On page 88 is a sample hand-drawn rating form, such as you can make on any lined paper. Notice that this smoker had his first cigarette at 7:30 on this particular morning, while at the breakfast table. He rated it 5, meaning that he wanted it very much. He marked off al-

THE TECHNIQUES OF SUCCESS

Day				
	Time	Activity	Desire	
1	7:30	Breakfast	5	
2	8:20	Driving	4	
3	8:50	Driving	2	
4				
5				
6				
7				
8				
9				
10				
11				
12				
13				
14				
15				
16				
17				
18				
19				
20				

most the entire right-hand part of the cigarette, indicating that he smoked it all the way down to the filter.

He smoked his next two cigarettes while driving his car. He wanted Cigarette Number Two a lot, though not as much as he'd wanted his breakfast cigarette, and he smoked all of it. Cigarette Number Three was different: he barely wanted it at all and smoked less than half of it.

The Rating Form

Maintain your rating form in this way with each cigarette you smoke, starting a new notebook page or form every day. Carry the form with you wherever you go, preferably wrapped around your cigarette pack (along with a pencil) and secured with a rubber band. At the end of each day, file the rating form carefully. You will refer to it often as your campaign progresses.

Every week, when you meet other smokers in your group, take your growing file of rating forms with you. Show them to your partner, study his, and discuss them. After a week you will begin to notice patterns emerging —patterns that you were probably never aware of before. As you'll see a little later, these patterns—and your knowledge of them—are of utmost importance in your climb to success.

. . .

But it's a damned nuisance, you say. *Every time I want a smoke, I've got to get out one of these forms and a pencil. It's embarrassing, too. When I do it in a restaurant or at work, people wonder.*

Ah. That's one of the main points. It's *meant* to be a damned nuisance.

The trouble with smoking, as we've pointed out before, is that it is too easy a habit to slide into. It's so easy that it becomes automatic after a while: almost a reflex action, often performed without thinking. You are beginning the process of throwing minor obstructions into this automatic machinery. If you handle the rating task faithfully and conscientiously, you will be forced to think seriously and long about each cigarette. Not long in terms of clock time: a few seconds, perhaps. But very long in comparison to the amount of thinking you used to do—which is to say, none.

A nuisance? Frankly, yes. But not an unmitigated nuisance. In the first place, it will happen less and less often as the weeks progress. In the second place, you will probably find it interesting. You'll learn things about your habit that never occurred to you before. You'll learn them because, for perhaps the first time, you're being forced to analyze your smoking complex in detail.

One thing you will probably notice almost instantly is that many of the cigarettes you smoke during the day—perhaps nearly a half—are 1's and 2's. They are cigarettes you barely want at all. They are the results of blind habit. You light them and smoke them automatically, like a robot, without thinking about them.

The very act of making out a rating form for a few days will quite probably cause you to stop smoking many or all of these 1's and 2's, these blindly automatic cigarettes. For the first time in your life you are thinking about them. The act of taking out your rating form and entering data on it will by itself render these cigarettes less automatic, and the enforced thinking will contribute to the process.

Thus, in this first stage of your campaign—within the first week or two—you will in all likelihood notice a big and virtually effortless drop in your cigarette consumption, perhaps a drop of as much as forty percent. Don't be surprised by this, and above all *don't expect the drop to continue at the same pace in the coming weeks.*

All that has happened in this first stage is that you have stopped smoking the cigarettes you really didn't

The Rating Form

want much, the automatic 1's and 2's. The cigarettes that are left are mainly 3's, 4's, and 5's. Your attack on these will take more time, thought, and effort.

As a matter of fact, you may notice as you pass into the more difficult second stage that your cigarette consumption goes back up slightly for a brief time. Don't let this discourage you. This happens to many smokers. Very few go to zero in a straight line; the majority take a zigzag course. This is especially true of the smoker who cuts his cigarette consumption by a big percentage in this first stage, right after starting to draw up his daily rating forms. He tends to get too complacent about this early and easy success; he thinks the rest of his campaign will be equally effortless. When he passes into the somewhat more demanding second stage, he tends to be disappointed momentarily by the apparent slowdown in his progress. Feeling gloomy, he smokes a few cigarettes more than he did at the height of his exhilaration in the first stage.

Expect to backslide occasionally. It's normal and natural. Don't worry about it.

Eventually and without a great deal of effort, mainly by use of your rating forms and social pressures, you will drop to a level of twenty or fewer cigarettes a day. This will happen sometime in the second stage of your campaign. (Your timetable in this movement through the stages is explained in detail, of course, in Part IV of the book.) From this point on, your rating forms will show that you are smoking only those cigarettes that you really want. All the blindly automatic cigarettes—the robot's cigarettes—are gone; only the 3's through 5's remain.

At this point, the rating forms phase into another kind

THE TECHNIQUES OF SUCCESS

of use. By showing the time and activity associated with each of your remaining cigarettes, the forms give you a graphic picture of your basic smoking complex. They show precisely what your sub-habits are. Armed with this essential knowledge, you then move into the third and final stage of your campaign.

These various uses of the rating form will be explained fully at the appropriate times. At the moment, we only want to impress on you the importance of the forms —the absolute necessity of maintaining them every day, meticulously, throughout your campaign.

To give you an idea of what to expect when you actually commit yourself to the program and begin making out your first day's rating form, here are two typical case studies from our files. Each study is based on one rating form maintained by a smoker in one day's smoking. One of the smokers was a man going through a normal working day at his office. The other was a woman smoking her way through a typical weekend day. Each had been in the Smoke Watchers program for about one week at the time.

A Thursday in the Life of Joe R.
   Cigarette #1: 6:45 A.M.
   Joe smoked this one immediately on arising. On his rating form he first rated it a 5, then crossed that number out and put down 4 instead. When we asked him about this later, he said his first thought had been that he wanted the cigarette badly because he hadn't had one during the eight hours or so he'd been asleep. But then he realized, even before lighting the cigarette, that his

The Rating Form

throat was sore and his mouth gummy from yesterday's smoking. So he demoted the cigarette from a 5 to a 4.

#2: 7:20 A.M.

Joe had brushed his teeth, shaved, and dressed, and now he had another cigarette as his wife got breakfast started. He didn't enjoy it much and knew in advance that he wasn't going to enjoy it much. The taste of toothpaste was still in his mouth and the mixture of this with tobacco smoke was not pleasant. He rated the cigarette a 2 and knew, even as he wrote the number on his form, that he wouldn't smoke more than half the cigarette. It occurred to him that he probably wouldn't smoke this particular cigarette at all tomorrow. For years he had lit this before-breakfast cigarette automatically, half-consciously, like a robot blindly obeying pre-programed commands. The very act of using the rating form, the very existence of the form, was now about to delete this senseless, joyless, automatic cigarette from Joe's smoking sequence.

#3: 7:45 A.M.

Joe smoked this cigarette with his after-breakfast coffee and unequivocally rated it a 5. He wanted it a lot and enjoyed it thoroughly.

The mere act of using the rating form wouldn't effortlessly kill this cigarette, as was happening with Cigarette #2. What the rating form would do—in fact, had already done—was to isolate and identify this breakfast-coffee cigarette as a separate sub-habit—a strong sub-habit that Joe would have to attack by itself at a later stage in his campaign.

Joe had been vaguely aware for years that this and other sub-habits existed in his daily smoking. He knew each day's smoking was much like every other day's; he realized the same patterns were repeated day after day; he always smoked at certain hours and in certain recurring situations, such as that of drinking coffee after breakfast. He had known this but had never analyzed it or attempted to elucidate it in detail. Now, with his rating forms, he was beginning to get an extremely clear picture of what his daily smoking patterns were. After using the forms for a week, he could see his breakfast-coffee cigarette standing out starkly as a repeated daily episode. The cigarette was entered on every day's form, and every day it was a 5.

#4: 8:15 A.M.

This one was smoked during Joe's drive to his job. He rated it a 3.

The drive normally took about forty-five minutes. Before committing himself to the Smoke Watchers program and starting his rating forms, Joe had virtually chainsmoked during this drive. It was a rare morning on which he didn't smoke at least three cigarettes while at the wheel of his car. But the cigarettes had all been automatic ones like Cigarette #2; Joe had lit them with the same unthinking, robotlike movements he used in working the controls of his car. Immediately on starting his rating forms and being forced to think about these cigarettes, he had stopped smoking all but one of them. He had realized he didn't want them; they were only a nuisance, interfering with his driving and spraying his suit with a snow of ashes. Now he smoked only one cigarette during the morning drive, enjoying it moderately.

He could not, of course, mark his rating form while in the process of taking out, lighting, and smoking this

The Rating Form

cigarette. He marked the form when he arrived at his office building and parked the car.

#5: 9:20 A.M.

This cigarette came as Joe sat down at his desk and mentally prepared himself for his day's work. He rated it a 2 and smoked only half of it. His past days' rating forms showed that he always lit a cigarette at this time, seldom smoked it all the way down, and always rated it as either a 2 or a 3. It was a minor sub-habit, one that he could probably attack and defeat at a later stage with little trouble.

#6: 10:05 A.M.

At a conference with his boss and several of his colleagues (Joe was an industrial salesman), he smoked another cigarette and rated it a 3.

#7: 10:40 A.M.

The midmorning coffee break. Joe rated this cigarette a 4 and smoked it all the way down. Idly flipping through his past few days' rating forms, he noted that he always smoked with coffee and always rated the cigarette high. He had never thought about this before. Apparently, with him, smoking with coffee was a major sub-habit. He might have to break it into small, manageable segments when the time came to attack it, rather than trying to defeat the entire coffee sub-habit at once. He might have to attack the coffee-break cigarette first, then the breakfast-coffee cigarette, and so on. But there would be plenty of time to think about this and plan his attack. He made a mental note to bring up the problem next time he was with others in his benevolent pressure group and particularly when he talked to his partner. Somebody might have some suggestions. He seemed to remember hearing his partner talk about some kind of difficulty over a coffee-break cigarette.

#8: 11:50 A.M.

A cigarette just before the lunch hour. Not a particularly compelling one: Joe hesitated over the rating, finally putting it down as a 3.

#9: 12:25 P.M.

Walking to lunch in a diner across the street from his office building, Joe lit his ninth cigarette of the day, pausing on a sidewalk to rate the cigarette a 3. He smoked about three-quarters of it. He put it out when he sat down in the booth with three lunch companions, none of whom smoked.

Joe had always felt uneasy when smoking near nonsmokers. The smoke bothered them, got in their eyes, interfered with the aroma of their food. He knew his lunchtime friends, though too considerate to say so, thought his habit an unnecessary nuisance. He would be glad when he, too, was a nonsmoker.

#10: 1:15 P.M.

Joe had another cigarette with his after-lunch coffee. It went down on his rating form as a 4. He thought: *This coffee sub-habit may be the worst one I have.*

His fellow lunchers watched him mark his rating form but considerately made no comments. He had asked them to leave him alone with his campaign, on the basis outlined in Chapter 10. Two of them were among those lucky millions who have never smoked; they didn't quite understand what Joe was going through but respected his wishes, being intelligent men. The other luncher was an ex-smoker. He understood fully what Joe was trying to do. He had, in fact, helped convince the others that they

The Rating Form

should refrain from kidding Joe or needling him or otherwise amusing themselves at his expense.

#11: 1:30 P.M.

Another cigarette while walking back to the office. Joe rated it a 2, smoked less than half of it, wondered why he had bothered to light it in the first place.

#12: 2:05 P.M.

Joe had wandered around the office for a while, chatting with fellow employees. Now, as he sat down at his desk and prepared for an afternoon of calling customers and prospects on the phone, he lit a cigarette. He rated it a 2. It occurred to him that this one was similar to his fifth cigarette of the day, which he had lit when he first sat down at his desk that morning. Both cigarettes came at times when he was mentally preparing to plunge into some demanding session of work. In his mind he labeled them "procrastination cigarettes." He had identified another sub-habit.

#13: 3:00 P.M.

The midafternoon coffee break—with a cigarette, of course. Joe rated it a 4 and smoked all of it.

#14: 3:50 P.M.

Joe was called into a sales meeting. He smoked a cigarette that he labeled a 3. He recognized it as similar to the cigarette he had smoked at a conference that morning. Here was still another sub-habit. For some reason he felt a need for a cigarette whenever conferring with other people. Why? To conceal nervousness? To appear profound and thoughtful? He wasn't sure, but he resolved to bring the question up with his fellow anti-cigarette campaigners next time he saw them.

#15: 4:40 P.M.

He smoked a cigarette that he didn't really want—a robot's cigarette. He called it a 2. Before starting his campaign, he recalled, he had smoked several such cigarettes in this part of the afternoon. Most had been rated as 1's. He doubted that he would smoke any tomorrow.

#16: 5:20 P.M.

A cigarette just before leaving the office. He didn't enjoy this one much either. He rated it 2 and smoked only half of it.

#17: 5:45 P.M.

Joe had another cigarette as he left the office and walked to his car. Rating: 3. It seemed to him that this cigarette might resemble the one he had smoked while walking to lunch. Both cigarettes came when he was leaving his place of work and heading for a period of relaxation. Was this still another sub-habit? He determined to study his rating forms with care after he had gone through another week, seeking repetitions of this apparent pattern. Did he smoke end-of-work cigarettes on weekends too? Or on days when he was out selling "on the road" instead of in his office? He didn't know the answers but knew he was going to find them. Joe was learning a lot about himself as a smoker.

#18: 6:05 P.M.

Driving home, he smoked a 3. As in the mornings, he had formerly chainsmoked while driving his car. Now the robot's cigarettes were gone. He wondered how easy it would be to kill this sub-habit altogether. Quite easy, he suspected. He looked forward to moving into the final stage of his campaign when he would attack his sub-habits one by one.

#19: 6:15 P.M.

Caught in a rush-hour traffic jam, Joe smoked another

The Rating Form

cigarette out of sheer frustration. Rating: 2. He was normally an easygoing man who tended to take life as it came, and he didn't recognize "frustration cigarettes" as a major sub-habit in his particular smoking complex. But it might be, he thought, that frustration occasionally increased his wish to smoke—not every day, just sometimes. He would have to think about this and talk it over with his fellow campaigners.

#20: 6:55 P.M.

Joe and his wife had a cocktail before dinner. This cigarette went down on his rating form as a 5. Like many Smoke Watchers, Joe knew the cocktail cigarette would take a lot of effort to beat.

#21: 7:10 P.M.

A second cocktail cigarette, rated 3 and smoked only two-thirds of the way down.

#22: 8:15 P.M.

After-dinner coffee and a 4, smoked all the way down.

#23: 9:30 P.M.

Watching a television show, Joe had his twenty-third cigarette of the day. He rated it a 3. He put it out, half-smoked, when one of the American Cancer Society's anti-cigarette commercials appeared on the screen. A week ago, he reflected, he had habitually smoked many robot's cigarettes while watching TV.

#24: 10:45 P.M.

Joe had his last cigarette of the day with a can of beer just before he went to bed. He called this cigarette a 3.

He glanced down his day's rating form one last time. He noted its remarkable similarity to the form he had filled out the day before, and the day before that. Never before had he realized how strong were the habit patterns that made up his smoking complex. Every day he smoked the same cigarettes at about the same times, for the same reasons, with the same degrees of enjoyment.

He also noted that there were no 1's on his day's form. All these had vanished effortlessly.

Today was Thursday. In two more days, Joe would begin his second weekend of maintaining the rating forms. He wondered whether his habit patterns on the coming Saturday and Sunday would mirror those of the previous weekend. He was virtually certain they would.

A Saturday in the Life of Anne McC.

Cigarette #1: 8:10 A.M.

Anne McC., who never smoked before breakfast, had her first cigarette of the day with her after-breakfast coffee. She rated it a 3. If she could have smoked it in peace, alone, she might have rated it higher. As things were, she smoked it with her four youngest children eating messily around her, bickering and shouting. Her husband had arisen earlier with their oldest daughter and had gone out, grumbling, to drive to a Girl Scout campsite. He would come home later in a bad mood. Anne sighed. It was going to be one of those Saturdays.

#2: 8:50 A.M.

The phone rang and it was one of her neighbors calling to discuss plans for a church picnic the following weekend. Anne went through an automatic sequence of movements: she tucked the phone against her left shoulder so as to free both hands, reached for her cigarettes and matches with her right hand, tapped the pack on the table to shake a cigarette loose, started to probe into the pack with her left forefinger. Only when her finger came up against the rating form that she had rubber-

The Rating Form

banded over the opening did she become conscious of what she was doing. She had gone through the sequence like a robot, without actually realizing she was doing it. With her, telephone cigarettes represented a major sub-habit.

The phone conversation lasted nearly half an hour. Before committing herself to the Smoke Watchers program, Anne might have smoked two or three cigarettes automatically during this time. As it was, she smoked one, rating it a 4.

#3: 10:00 A.M.

Anne smoked her third cigarette while driving to a supermarket with two of her children. (The other two were playing with neighbors' kids.) She rated the cigarette a 2, but she smoked it all the way down anyway. Anne was one of those smokers who, perhaps because of some deep-seated frugality, hated to throw away a partly smoked cigarette. When she lit one, she finished it no matter how little she was enjoying it. Possibly, she thought, this obsession was a kind of sub-habit in itself. It might prove useful, in a later stage of her campaign, deliberately to smoke at least some of the day's cigarettes only halfway down. She made a mental note to talk with her fellow campaigners about this odd question.

#4: 10:50 A.M.

Waiting in a long line at the supermarket checkout counter, Anne lit another cigarette and rated it 2. Her past week's rating forms had revealed to her that she always smoked when nervous, irritable, frustrated, or generally unhappy. She hated waiting in line at supermarkets. It seemed to her that, if she was about to hand the supermarket company a lot of money, the least the company could do was make the process quick and painless. Standing in line made her mad, and so she smoked. She didn't enjoy the cigarette; in fact her rating forms showed that she didn't enjoy any of her frustration cigarettes. None was ever rated higher than 3. And yet she felt compelled to smoke them. Why? She resolved to talk it over with her partner.

Some psychologists have paid special attention to this phenomenon of frustration smoking. Some smokers—for example, Joe R.—smoke mainly to enhance or accompany pleasurable feelings, as when drinking or relaxing after work. These have been called "positive-affect" smokers. Others, like Anne McC., are predominantly "negative-affect" smokers: they more often light up to relieve painful or unpleasant feelings. The majority of smokers probably represent a little of both. Each can analyze his own smoking complex in detail, of course, through careful attention to daily ratings.

#5: 11:25 A.M.

On the phone again, Anne smoked a 4.

#6: 11:50 A.M.

All the children were out of the house temporarily, playing around the neighborhood. Alone and enjoying her first peaceful moment of the day, Anne made a cup of tea, phoned her best friend for a long chat, and smoked a 5.

#7: 12:30 P.M.

Anne's husband was home from the Girl Scout camp, predictably grumpy because his Saturday was now half shot. He and Anne had been invited to a cocktail party that evening and he spent the lunch hour explaining why he didn't want to go. Anne, knowing he would enjoy himself hugely when he finally got there, let him grumble

The Rating Form

and smoked a cigarette so she wouldn't have to talk much. She rated it a 2.

#8: 1:20 P.M.

She smoked a cigarette while listing an order of children's clothes from the Sears, Roebuck catalogue, and then . . .

#9: 1:45 P.M.

. . . another while phoning in the order. She rated both these cigarettes 3's. It occured to her a few minutes later, while glancing down her day's rating form, that she tended to smoke whenever she was spending money. Her husband's income was adequate but not large enough to free the family of money worries. It upset her to see money going out in large chunks: twenty dollars for a supermarket order, forty dollars or so for an order of children's clothes. Perhaps in her case, she thought, the "money cigarette" was a sub-habit in its own right—a category of frustration or irritation cigarettes. She remembered hearing one of her fellow campaigners mention this one day and resolved to ask about it next time they ran into each other.

#10: 2:30 P.M.

One of Anne's little girls was going to a birthday party, and the other children were jealous. There were squabbles and bitter tears as the small socialite put on her frilly party dress. Anne smoked a cigarette to calm herself, rating it 2.

#11: 3:15 P.M.

Driving to the birthday party and still feeling edgy, she smoked another 2. It seemed to her that she might be able to divide her driving cigarettes into two minor sub-habits: irritable driving cigarettes and just plain bored driving cigarettes.

#12: 4:05 P.M.

She took the other children to an ice-cream stand to soothe their disappointment over the birthday party. But they squabbled anyway, and one of them dropped ice cream on the car's freshly cleaned upholstery. Anne smoked a 3.

#13: 5:00 P.M.

The birthday party was over. Anne chatted briefly with the hostess mother and was tempted to smoke while doing so, but refrained. She didn't want to go through the trouble of explaining what the rating form was all about. After using the form for a week, she was used to keeping it wrapped around her cigarette pack; the form was beginning to be a sub-habit by itself. Anne didn't want to cheat herself by hiding or ignoring the form, even if only once in a while. Rather than do that, she preferred not to smoke. She postponed her thirteenth cigarette of the day until she was driving her daughter home in the car. She felt relatively relaxed. She called the cigarette a 3.

#14: 6:30 P.M.

Anne had not smoked while she and her husband were dressing for the cocktail party. At six o'clock she had kept her regular telephone appointment with her partner, another housewife. They had talked mainly about the difficulty of holding down one's cigarette consumption while at a party. The partner suggested that Anne stay close to the potato chips, peanuts, or perhaps some sort of low-calorie nibbles that might be provided. Anne had automatically reached for a cigarette while on the phone, but had encountered the rating form and put the pack down again, feeling that it was ridiculous, somehow, to smoke while talking to one's partner. She

The Rating Form

had refrained from smoking until she and her husband were in the car, driving to the party. She rated this cigarette a 3.

#15: 7:20 P.M.

Anne nibbled cucumber slices and other goodies for half an hour before lighting her first cigarette at the party. She wanted it a lot and called it a 5. She went into the bathroom to mark her rating form so she wouldn't have to answer questions about it.

#16: 7:55 P.M.

Several times, Anne found her hand reaching automatically into her clutch bag for cigarettes. She would have smoked a cigarette every ten or fifteen minutes at the party if it hadn't been for the rating form that was wrapped around her pack. The existence of the form precluded this robotlike smoking. Anne's second cigarette at the party was a 3.

#17: 8:20 P.M.

Somebody offered her a cigarette. She had had three drinks and was no longer totally in control of herself. She accepted the cigarette and did not enter it on her rating form until much later. She recalled it as a 2. It was a robot's cigarette, smoked mechanically. The tobacco taste did not mix well with the taste of cucumbers and onion dip.

#18: 8:45 P.M.

Riding home in the car with her husband, she lit another cigarette that she didn't enjoy at all. It was a 1. Her mouth tasted bad. She knew she was going to have a mean cigarette-and-alcohol hangover the next morning, but she reflected that it might have been much worse. She had smoked only four cigarettes since arriving at the party. Without her rating form to interrupt the periodic movement of reaching for a cigarette, she might have smoked ten or more cigarettes at the party without even realizing she was lighting them.

#19: 9:35 P.M.

Anne and her husband had a quick supper of leftovers and coffee. Neither was very hungry. Anne smoked her last cigarette of the day with the coffee, called it a 3, and yearned for the future day when she would not want cigarettes at all.

She was progressing well, however, she thought as she went to bed. For several years she had smoked somewhere between one-and-a-half and two packs—thirty to forty cigarettes—a day. Nearly half of these, apparently, had been robot's cigarettes. She hadn't realized it, hadn't even thought about it until the rating form forced her to do so. In one week of using the rating form, she had effortlessly killed most of these mechanically smoked cigarettes.

She knew the next stages of her campaign would be more demanding. But, as she told us when we went over this Saturday's rating form with her, "I was looking forward to the next stages. I was already thinking of myself as a nonsmoker-in-training."

12 ※ Counting and Charting

At the same time as you begin maintaining your rating form, you should also begin charting your progress week by week.

This is done more or less mechanically. You begin by making a record of the number of cigarettes you smoke each day. Simply look at each day's rating form and see how many cigarettes are listed on it. Then enter this number in the appropriate place on a daily counting chart like the one on page 108. You can use this chart itself if you like—or else make your own similar chart.

Try to talk to your benevolent pressure group after you have Week Number One filled out, including the week's average (which you calculate simply by totaling the seven days' consumption and dividing by seven).

In the group's presence—not when you're alone—you fill in the last box of Week Number One: your quota for next week. It's essential that you do this in public, with the whole group watching and listening. You announce to the group, "This week my average was X, and next week I'm going down to X minus 5." If you do

Daily Counting Chart

WEEK	SUN	MON	TUES	WED	THURS	FRI	SAT	TOTAL	DAILY AVERAGE	NEXT WEEK'S QUOTA
1										
2										
3										
4										
5										
6										
7										
8										
9										
10										
11										
12										
13										
14										
15										
16										
17										
18										
19										
20										
21										
22										
23										
24										
25										
26										

Counting and Charting

this while you're alone, you will lose the benefit of the group's benevolent pressure.

What should your "Next Week's Quota" be? Smokers vary in the speed at which they reduce their consumption. As we've said, there is often a very sharp drop in the first week or two, followed by a leveling off. As a general rule of thumb, throughout most of your campaign, a reduction of ten percent to fifteen percent a week is reasonable. Thus, if your average in a certain week is twenty cigarettes a day, you can plan in the next week to reduce the level by two or three. Don't feel bound by this general rule, however. In some weeks you may bring about a much sharper reduction, while in others you may have less success or may even backslide temporarily.

You should maintain your daily counting chart faithfully, seven days a week. Meanwhile, you should also be filling in the weekly progress chart on page 110.

At the end of each week, when you've figured out your week's average on the daily counting chart, make a dot at the appropriate place on the grid in the weekly progress chart. Connect this dot with a line to the previous week's dot. This will give you a clear, graphic picture of your progress toward nonsmoking. You are aiming, of course, for the bottom line of the weekly progress chart: the Zero Line.

• • •

It's essential that you maintain both the daily and weekly charts with care, as well as the rating form. You may think all this chart-making is a waste of time and perhaps a little silly. "I don't need to write down a lot of numbers and draw lines on charts."

My Weekly Progress Chart

AMOUNT OF CIGARETTES

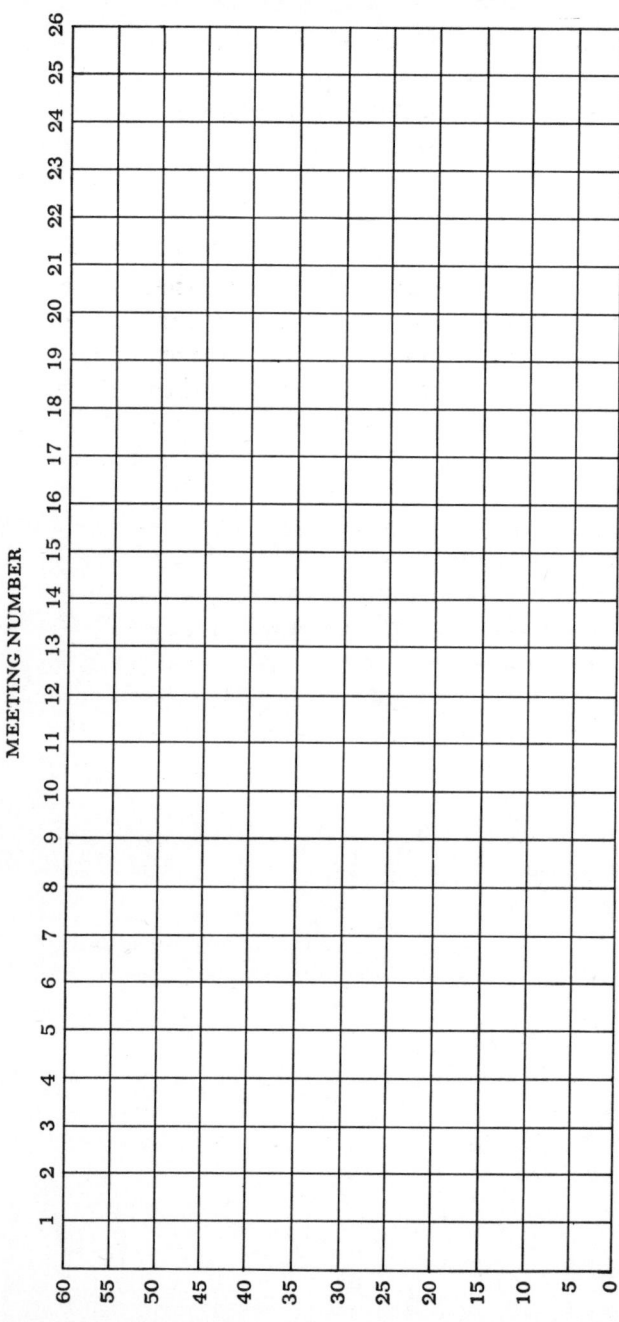

MEETING NUMBER

As of each meeting date, enter average daily cigarette consumption for previous week on the above chart.

Counting and Charting

Not so. You *do* need to go through this kind of exercise. For this business of counting cigarettes and making charts is an important early part of the habit-breaking process. It isn't just an exercise in grade-school arithmetic.

Until now, you've been smoking cigarettes automatically. Often, without really thinking, you've lit one after another after another like a robot. What you are doing now, with your group's subtle pressure backing you up, is beginning to put deliberate interruptions in the way of the habit. Instead of smoking automatically, you are now going to think about each cigarette as you pull it out of the pack, as you light it and smoke it and put it out.

The chart-making exercise is designed to start making you do just that. From now on, when you smoke a cigarette, you will be counting it: "This is my seventeeth today . . . my twenty-fourth . . ." You are beginning to interrupt the chain of automatic actions that is so important a part of your smoking problem. Your conscious mind is starting to insinuate itself into an area of your life to which it has previously paid too little attention.

So maintain your charts and forms faithfully. You may consider them a minor nuisance at first. However, as you continue through the weeks, you'll probably find the chart-making exercise more and more interesting. "It's a crazy kind of thrill," one of our clients once told us, "to see the line on the weekly chart plunging down toward that old Zero Line."

The Zero Line. You'll get there one day too.

13 ❧ *The Habit List*

We've pointed out before that the so-called "cigarette habit" isn't just one habit, but a series of sub-habits. Your next step is to begin isolating these sub-habits and attacking them one by one.

This step comes after you've come down to or below the level of twenty cigarettes a day. There wasn't much point in trying to do this while you were still smoking more than that. The task would have been too complicated. Now it will be relatively simple. What's more, we think you'll find it interesting.

The act of rating and counting all your cigarettes—*thinking* about them individually—helped you abandon all those that were entrely automatic: the robot's cigarettes, the ones you didn't particularly want but smoked unthinkingly in a kind of reflex action. All right. You are now smoking twenty or fewer cigarettes that you still seem to want, even after thinking about them. What you must do now is study your past seven days' rating forms and analyze each of these remaining cigarettes.

You will almost certainly find that you were engaged in some particular activity as you smoked each one. There were morning-coffee cigarettes, driving-in-the-car cigarettes, cocktail cigarettes, talking-on-the-phone ciga-

The Habit List

rettes, and so on. Each of these cigarettes *is a habit by itself*.

Take a sheet of paper and analyze your past week's smoking in the manner shown on the following page.

List every one of your recognizable smoking habits, and then enter the daily average number of cigarettes represented by each habit. For instance, you may find that you smoked an average of three cigarettes a day last week while talking on the phone, one a day while lounging around after breakfast, and so on.

Notice how each number tends to stay roughly the same from day to day. You smoke three or four telephone cigarettes *every day*, two or three cocktail cigarettes *every day*. Each sub-habit is etched deeply into your mental processes.

When you have analyzed your sub-habits in this way and are fairly sure you know what your habit pattern is, decide on one sub-habit that you want to attack. *Just one.* The telephone-cigarette habit, say. Or the after-lunch cigarette. Attack this habit alone. Cut out this particular cigarette, and don't try to attack any other sub-habit until you feel quite comfortable about the first one.

To help you attack your sub-habits, you'll find on the next few pages a list of what we've found to be the most common ones, along with some suggestions for what you can do to beat each of them. Don't rely on our suggestions alone, however. You should talk over each sub-habit with other smokers who are also reaching for success; get their suggestions too.

· · ·

The wake-up cigarette. Some smokers feel a strong wish for a cigarette immediately on arising in the morn-

HABIT LIST	NUMBER OF CIGARETTES

Wake-up cigarette _____
After breakfast _____
While driving _____
While walking on the street _____
While on the telephone _____
When talking to someone _____
At scheduled work breaks _____
Before lunch _____
After lunch _____
After shopping in a public store _____
In the bathroom _____
While waiting _____
Midafternoon _____
After accomplishing some task (as a reward) _____
After participating in some sport _____
After cocktails _____
While watching T.V. _____
Before dinner _____
After dinner _____
During exciting moments while being a spectator
    to sports, movies, plays, etc. _____
While reading _____
With nightcap _____
After sex _____
With insomnia _____
Other _____
_____
_____
_____
_____
_____
_____
_____

The Habit List

ing—sometimes before even getting out of bed. If this cigarette is one of your habits, try any of the following suggestions:

- Drink a glass of orange juice immediately on arising. Many smokers find that the taste of orange juice doesn't mix with tobacco smoke; one diminishes the wish for and pleasure in the other.
- Arrange to have a morning newspaper delivered to your home, and read it on arising or with breakfast. One Smoke Watcher told us the stock-market quotations became his personal substitute for the wake-up cigarette he used to smoke. He became fascinated by the market and went on to make a lot of money in it.
- Reserve some special treat for yourself later in the morning. For example, include in your breakfasts from now on a food that you haven't usually eaten until now. Some smokers find this makes them hurry through washing and dressing in the mornings. Instead of brooding about the missing wake-up cigarette, they hurry to breakfast.

The coffee cigarette. For many smokers, a cigarette smoked with the first cup of coffee in the morning—or with any cup of coffee—is a Number 5. To beat it:

- Change to tea or some other drink.
- Change your way of flavoring coffee. For example, drink it without sugar if you've used sugar in the past.
- Munch a tea biscuit with your coffee, or a roll, or a muffin, or anything else that you enjoy the taste of.

The after-breakfast cigarette. This could be a coffee cigarette, or it could be simply a cigarette smoked while

THE TECHNIQUES OF SUCCESS

ambling around, preparing for the day ahead. Some smokers find, on coming free, that there is a "dead" period after breakfast. In this period, lasting maybe half an hour, they habitually did nothing in the past but smoke a cigarette or two and mentally shift into gear for the day's work. To beat this habit:

- Get into the habit of reading. Carry a paperback book with you wherever you go and open it whenever there is a dead period in your day.
- Change your schedule so that the dead period no longer exists. One smoker of our acquaintance did this by showering, shaving, and dressing after breakfast instead of before. Another did it by walking to a more distant bus stop than the one he'd previously used on his way to work. The extra twenty-minute walk filled the after-breakfast dead period and, so he reported, "helped me do my morning thinking and planning. It was better than sitting around smoking a cigarette. I missed the cigarette on the first couple of days, but by the end of the week I was glad it was gone."

The driver's cigarette. This is the one you used to smoke while driving a car. Some smokers believe this cigarette helps them relax at the wheel and makes them better drivers, although there is no factual basis for the belief. (Smoking at the wheel is dangerous, in fact. The smoker may drop his cigarette on the car seat or may burn his fingers at some critical time—and the result could be an accident. In some countries, it is illegal to smoke while driving.) To beat this cigarette:

- Turn on the car radio, or carry a portable radio if there is none in the car.

The Habit List

- Seek passengers to ride with you. Talking to them will help you relax. One smoker, an insurance executive, had habitually driven to work by himself in the mornings, and the cigarette he had smoked on the way was a tough one in his book. To beat it, he organized a car pool among other men traveling the same route. Another smoker, a housewife, had to drive a long distance twice a week to take her daughter to music lessons. She found the long ride boring and depressing. To beat the driver's cigarette, she began inviting her daughter's friends to ride along. They sang songs and played arithmetical and other games in the car. "It sounds silly," the housewife told us, "and some of my neighbors thought I was nuts. What woman in her right mind would take kids in a car when she didn't have to? But it made the ride interesting for me, and by the time the music lessons ended that summer, I was completely free of the driver's cigarette."
- Chew a sugarless gum or eat a hard candy while driving.

The waiting cigarette. You smoked this cigarette while cooling your heels in a doctor's waiting room, or standing in line at a supermarket checkout counter. At times like this there sometimes seems to be nothing else to do except smoke. But this habit can be beaten easily by:
- Pulling out your paperback novel.
- Eating a hard candy or lozenge.
- Watching others smoking and rehearsing in your mind all the benefits you have and they lack.

The midmorning cigarette. This is the one many smokers associate with the midmorning break from work. It can be a tough one to beat, for the association is built into our very culture. Men who have served in the U.S. armed forces at any time in the past thirty years may recall the standard midmorning invitation from an officer: "Take ten. . . . Light up." It was more than a suggestion; it was almost a command. Many men learned to smoke in this situation. To win:

- Phone your buddy or partner. The midmorning break is an excellent time for this daily contact, for the chances are that you and your partner can arrange to take your breaks at the same time.
- Take a brief, brisk walk outdoors.
- Instead of or in addition to coffee, eat a lozenge or candy or a tart fruit, such as an apple.
- Stand up, take a glass of water and several deep breaths. Then sit down and relax in a comfortable chair for five minutes or so.

The pause-to-think cigarette. You may often have smoked this cigarette during conversations. Somebody asks you a question or says something requiring a response. Instead of asking for time to think, you cover your hesitation by lighting a cigarette. Breaking this particular habit is largely a matter of finding other ways to create a thinking pause without making it seem awkward:

- Stand up and look out the window.
- Doodle on a pad for a few seconds.
- Take a sip of your tea or coffee if you have any. Or stand up and get a drink of water and take a few deep breaths.

The Habit List

The telephone cigarette. This is the one you always used to light while dialing or after picking up the phone. Not many smokers find this a very tough habit to beat:
- Doodle on a pad.
- Change the physical position that you normally adopt while phoning. For instance, stand up if you've normally been seated. Change the hand with which you hold the receiver.
- Find some toy to play with as you phone. Anything will do: a paperclip that you can bend or twirl, a child's toy automobile that you can roll about on the tabletop.
- Have a pitcher of cold water handy, and a glass.

The bathroom cigarette. The late actor Robert Taylor, a smoker who died of cancer, is reported to have remarked once that the only real peace and solitude he ever enjoyed in this crowded, urbanized age was when he was in a bathroom.

The topic is perhaps indelicate, but the purpose of this book is to help you become a nonsmoker. We are talking about life and death. Measured against this purpose, the delicacy or indelicacy of a topic seems to us irrelevant.

For many smokers, as for Robert Taylor, the bathroom cigarette is a Number 5. This represents possibly the only time in our day when we are unlikely to be disturbed by anyone, for any reason. The rare privacy and solitude are enjoyable, and cigarettes can become associated with the experience. To win:
- Deliberately seek some other place and time in which you can enjoy a daily period of uninterrupted and inviolable solitude—even a brief period. One Smoke Watchers' client, a frantically busy New York executive, did

so by deliberately taking a roundabout route each morning and evening between his office and his commuter train. He sought coffee shops where he was not known and where nobody from his world of work would be likely to appear. "I'd sit there for ten minutes or so twice a day with a glass of iced tea or something, just thinking how great it was that nobody would come up and talk to me or ask me to do anything. It worked. I enjoyed these periods so much, in fact, that I've since expanded them. Once a week, no matter what's happening at the office, no matter how much I think I'm needed, I sneak off by myself at noontime and go to a restaurant where nobody knows me and have lunch alone. Everybody needs at least some solitude in his day. I used to think I needed a cigarette to help me find this peace, but it turns out I don't."

The before-lunch cigarette. This is similar to the midmorning cigarette: it's associated with a break in the day's work. To win:

• Make some kind of change in your lunch routine. If you habitually eat at the same cafeteria, find another place. If you eat at home, seek a new menu or take yourself out to eat once in a while. The idea is to make lunch itself an interesting meal, so that the anticipation will help you forget the cigarette you used to smoke out of sheer boredom. "Lunch was always the most boring meal of the day for me," one housewife told us, "and I guess it is for many people. I'd eat the same old grilled cheese sandwich or tunafish salad every day, or if it wasn't that it'd be leftovers from supper the night be-

The Habit List

fore." This particular woman, on coming down to about five cigarettes a day, organized a lunch club among some of her friends and neighbors, including two who were going through the Smoke Watchers program with her. Once a week they went out to eat at a restaurant, and on certain other days they met for lunch at each other's homes. "It got me through the midday slump," she told us. "I didn't need that before-lunch cigarette any more. I guess I'd been smoking it mainly because I was feeling bored, lonesome, and sorry for myself."

- The lunch hour is another good time for talking to your partner.
- Shortly before the meal, eat a hard candy or lozenge. As we'll explain later (Chapter 17), this is especially useful for those who are worried about gaining weight.

The after-lunch cigarette. Like the after-breakfast cigarette, this one is generally associated with a dead or idle period. To beat the habit:

- Establish a new after-lunch routine for yourself. For example, work on some aspect of your hobby for half an hour after the meal. The stock-market fan we mentioned before used this period to read financial tip sheets, corporate reports, and other material related to his newfound interest. "I promised myself I'd read at least one piece of market literature every day after lunch," he said. "I don't say it was always fascinating reading. Sometimes it was deadly boring. But it gave me the feeling of being informed, and now I'd feel lost without this period. The cigarette? I'm not interested in it any more. It would only get in the way." Other Smoke Watchers' clients have told us they use the postprandial period for taking walks, listening to music, reading the sports news, and (in one case) writing a play.

The midafternoon cigarette. This is a strange one. With some smokers it's a Number 1: one of the least pleasant and least wanted cigarettes of the day. ("By the time I smoked that one I was always headachy and tired, and my throat was raw and my mouth tasted like the bottom of a bird's cage," one woman recalled.) But with other smokers it's a Number 5. They feel it helps them renew their energy, which tends to reach a low ebb in many people at this time of day. A cigarette patently cannot renew anyone's energy, of course, but if a smoker feels this effect takes place, the cigarette may be a tough one for him. To beat it:
- Drink a glass of juice or a cup of tea or coffee, or eat a hard candy or lozenge.
- If you can do so conveniently, perform a few minutes of calisthenics. Or walk a few blocks briskly. Or stand up, stretch hard, and take five or ten slow, deep breaths. These activities will give you the quick toning-up effect that you once sought from a cigarette.

The cocktail cigarette. You smoked this cigarette whenever you had an alcoholic drink of any kind, at any time, in any situation. For many smokers this is the toughest one of all.

One problem, of course, lies in the fact that alcohol relaxes the inhibitions and usually diminishes normal self-control. People who are drinking do all kinds of foolish

The Habit List

things that they wouldn't do when sober. They drive recklessly, they flirt too openly with one another's spouses, they get into fights. And they smoke. Moderate smokers become heavy smokers at cocktail parties. A man or woman who might normally smoke half a pack a day is likely to smoke an entire pack during a night's partying. An ex-smoker is in danger of falling back into the habit again when he drinks. All the mental and emotional balances that keep most of us mostly sane most of the time vanish under the influence of alcohol. There is nothing intrinsically wrong with this, of course. It can be great fun. But to one who is trying to come free from cigarettes, it is highly dangerous.

Another problem is that alcohol and cigarettes are very closely associated with each other in our culture. The association goes back into the teen-age years of many smokers. You probably tried your first alcoholic drink at about the same time, and in the same spirit of adventure and defiance and adulthood-seeking, as you tried your first cigarette. The two have been linked in your life ever since. Breaking them apart can be tough. To do it:

- Never carry your cigarettes or matches with you to a party, even if your current smoking level allows you to smoke that evening. Take only your rating form. If you allow yourself a cigarette, you must bum both it and the light. This necessity will, at least to some extent, counter the lapse of self-control that alcohol always brings.
- Phone your partner before any drinking session or during its early stages.
- If you're fairly sure hors d'oeuvres or other nibbles will be available where you're drinking, eat nothing beforehand. Then, when you begin to drink, nibble often.

(Note: this may make your stomach uncomfortable, but you'll feel better than if you had smoked. The world's worst hangovers come from the combination of drinking and heavy smoking. The need to nibble will diminish in any case once you're a confirmed nonsmoker.)

- If all else fails, abstain from drinking alcoholic beverages for a few months. We are aware this is hard advice to take, but in some cases it is the only way to win. Beer may be all right; many smokers find that the tastes of beer and tobacco don't mix particularly well. But for the smoker who finds the cocktail cigarette an unusually tough one, all other alcoholic drinks may be out for the time being.

The after-dinner cigarette. This one is associated with a contemplative time of day when you review the day's events by yourself, with friends, or with family members. It is the sundown cigarette: the one you smoked after the bulk of your day's work was done and you were preparing to relax for the evening. With most smokers it isn't a formidably tough cigarette to beat:

- Get up from the table more promptly. This may happen naturally, for you have more energy than when you were a heavier smoker. You won't feel that leaden weight of sundown fatigue. You'll be eager to get on with your hobbies, social events, and other interests.
- If you have nothing in particular to do on a certain evening and you feel nervous or at loose ends after dinner, go to a movie. The anticipation will carry you through the immediate after-dinner period, and the movie itself will keep you happy for the next two or three hours.

The Habit List

The nightcap cigarette. This is the one you smoked before going to bed. Only a small percentage of smokers find this one tough. If you're among them:

- Brush your teeth or use a mouthwash earlier in the evening—for example, after dinner instead of just before retiring. The clean taste of your mouth will argue against the thought of having a cigarette.
- Do your evening's reading in bed instead of in your armchair, and keep neither cigarettes nor ashtray anywhere near the bed. When you grow sleepy, simply turn out the light and lie down. You'll be too comfortable to get up and hunt for cigarettes.
- Use this hour to bring your various smoking charts up to date. Study them. In particular, review that day's rating form and ask yourself again why you smoked each cigarette listed. This activity will reinforce your interest in your own progress. You won't then want to light a cigarette and perhaps exceed your quota in the last hour of an otherwise successful day.

The after-sex cigarette. This is a curious one. Some smokers, even extremely heavy ones, feel no desire at all for a cigarette after a sexual episode. But some light and moderate smokers call this a Number 5. If you're among the latter, you may have found it tough to beat. This is especially true if your sex partner habitually smokes afterward. To win:

- If you're a talkative lovemaker (some are; some are silent), deliberately stop talking after the sex act and find some diplomatic way of making your partner do the same. Most people get pleasantly drowsy after sex and, if left to themselves, tend to fall asleep quickly or at least doze for a while. But the postcoital conversation wakes them up and then—if they're smokers—they may suddenly realize they want a cigarette. So don't talk afterward; just lie still with your eyes closed. If you miss the conversation, console yourself with the thought that you'll be able to resume it once you're a confirmed nonsmoker.

- If you don't become drowsy after sex, get out of bed and have a warm shower. Or—provided you've beaten the cocktail cigarette—have a glass of brandy.

The insomniac cigarette. You smoked this cigarette when you couldn't sleep and had to get up at 3 A.M. and prowl about the house. In all likelihood you'll have fewer sleepless nights as your smoking level approaches zero, for reasons that we've explained in previous chapters. For one thing, you'll be getting more exercise during the day. For another, your sexual activity will probably be increasing—and sex remains the world's best cure for insomnia. In spite of this, there may come a time when personal worries or some other factor will disturb your sleep. When that happens:

- Whatever you do, don't simply lie in bed staring at the ceiling. The insomniac mood is typically one of self-pity. The problems that are keeping you awake seem overwhelming; you feel very much alone and very, very sorry for yourself. In this mood, it's lamentably easy to talk yourself into smoking a consoling cigarette. So don't just lie there. Get up and find a book to read, or watch the late-late show on TV.
- If you sense that the problem will recur on other

The Habit List

nights, take a mild sleeping pill and go to bed an hour or so later than you otherwise would, until you're sleeping normally again. (But if you find you can't sleep normally without pills, see a doctor.)

The time-related cigarette. There may be a period of several hours during your typical day when you smoke cigarettes in a timed sequence rather than in relation to various activities. Your rating forms will tell you whether you're doing this. For example, in a typical afternoon of work, you may find you smoke a cigarette every forty-five minutes regardless of what activity you're engaged in at the time.

We've met smokers who appeared to smoke this way throughout the day. In other words, their whole smoking complex was related to time rather than activities—seemingly regulated by some mysterious inner clock. Such a smoker might have a cigarette every forty-five minutes from morning until night, and no particular cigarette would be rated much higher or lower than any others, whether it was smoked with coffee or while telephoning or in bed.

This kind of smoker is rather rare, however. Much more common is the smoker who lapses into a timed sequence during a certain, often brief, period of the day. Usually this period is one characterized by some degree of monotony. It may be a period of arduous work, or a period of simply sitting—traveling or commuting, for instance, or watching TV at night. You can think of such smoking as activity-related if you like—that is, you can call it your "commuting" or "TV-watching" sub-habit—

but you may find it more effective in a case like this to treat this portion of your smoking complex as a time-related sub-habit. To attack it:

- Deliberately stretch out the time sequence. That is, suppose your rating forms tell you that you usually smoke cigarettes at 8:00 P.M., 8:45, 9:30, and 10:15, regardless of whether you spend any particular evening watching TV or reading or listening to music. From now on, look at your watch before lighting cigarettes during this period. Stretch the forty-five minute sequence to an hour during the first week after you begin your attack on this particular sub-habit, then to an hour and fifteen minutes the second week, and so on.
- Or, alternatively, deliberately jumble the sequence. Try never to repeat a sequence in the same way two days running. For example, light up at 8:00 and 9:15 one night, at 8:15 and 9:00 the next, at 7:45 and 9:15 the next. This will gradually ease you out of the timing habit. The mysterious clock you carry in your head will ultimately stop giving you the periodic signal that says, "time for another cigarette."
- If possible, introduce some drastic and dramatic change into this characteristically monotonous period of the day. If your timed cigarettes come in the evenings and if you've habitually spent your evenings sitting around, get up and deliberately find something active to do. Play Ping-Pong, or join a glee club, or go bowling. If the timed sequence occurs during a work period when you can't introduce this kind of change, seek some way of breaking the period into shorter segments. For instance, if it's a period spent sitting at your desk from 2:00 P.M. to 5:30, arrange to stand up and take a brief

The Habit List

walk at 3:00, have a cup of tea or coffee at 4:00, phone your partner at 4:45.

. . .

As we've said, you should attack these sub-habits *one by one*. Go at your own pace. Don't pressure yourself too hard. Don't attack the telephone-cigarette habit until you feel perfectly at ease without your former pause-to-think cigarette.

You need make only one habit list. As you attack and defeat each habit, simply cross it off the list and turn your attention to the habits that still remain.

14 ❧ *The Smoker's Tic*

Another whole set of sub-habits is included in your smoking complex. This is the sequence of half-conscious, semiautomatic physical movements that you make in the course of smoking. You must defeat these, too, before you can defeat the complex.

What are these physical movements? In all likelihood you have never thought about them. You reach for your cigarettes in a certain place, you light one in a certain way, you hold it and smoke it in a certain way. You have been doing these things over and over again for years. If you've been smoking forty cigarettes a day for ten years, you've been through this set of motions nearly 150,000 times. The motions are so thoroughly practiced, so familiar, so nearly automatic that they themselves have become a part of your habit. They embody many characteristics of what medical men call a *tic*, an incessantly and compulsively repeated movement, such as a twitching of the eyebrows. A person afflicted with a tic can halt the movements when he thinks about them. They aren't actually involuntary, as are the twitchings and other movements in such illnesses as Parkinson's disease. A patient suffering from that disease cannot stop the motions no matter how hard he concentrates,

The Smoker's Tic

for his muscles aren't enough under his control. But a patient with an ordinary tic does have a measure of voluntary control. As long as he concentrates on his tic, *thinks about it,* he halts the motions. When his attention wanders to something else, the tic returns. It is *semivoluntary.*

In this sense, a tic is something like the act of breathing. Your chest and diaphragm muscles are under semivoluntary control. Most of the time you don't think about what they are doing. You don't need to. They continue to pull and push air in and out of your lungs automatically. But when you want to exert control over the breathing process—as in talking or singing, for example, or holding your breath under water, or smoking—you can do so. The muscles respond to your will as long as you exert some kind of volition on them. As soon as you stop exerting volition, the process returns to its involuntary, automatic mode.

The breathing habit is necessary, of course; without it you would not live. Facial and other muscular tics aren't necessary but aren't particularly harmful. They may embarrass the person afflicted but, as a rule, they don't in themselves affect his health or endanger his life. The smoking habit is the worst of all. It does affect health and endanger life.

The whole array of small movements and postures associated with your smoking can be thought of as a kind of multi-phased, or serial, tic. This serial tic is a component of your cigarette complex, and you've got to attack it simultaneously as you attack the other components or sub-habits. *You attack it by deliberately changing the movements.*

That is, you go on smoking at a gradually reducing

131

rate, in the way we've explained (and as outlined in detail in Part IV). You don't cut yourself off abruptly from cigarettes themselves as in the cold-turkey system. Instead, you divorce the cigarette complex from the associated serial tic.

In Chapter 5 we gave you some of the reasons why we aren't entirely in favor of the cold-turkey route for all smokers. Now we'll give you another reason. The cold-turkey quitter divorces himself from the cigarettes and the tic at the same time. Consciously or not, he misses both: the smoking itself and (exactly like a person afflicted with a muscular tic) the endlessly repeated series of familiar, comforting movements. He may not realize he is missing the movements, but usually he is. Often, without thinking, he will reach in his pocket for the cigarettes that used to be there. He may even go so far as to pull out matches and strike one and lift it to his face, only to realize with surprise and embarrassment that there is no cigarette in his mouth to be lit. He may be made uncomfortable for weeks because he doesn't know what to do with his hands. Dozens of times a day, this discomfort reminds him of cigarettes. His habituated body urges him to go back to the comfortable rut it used to know. All too often, in the end, he does.

This is why we urge you to get rid of the tic first, while you are still smoking. Get used to life without those familiar motions. Then, by the time you reach the Zero Line on your weekly progress chart, you will no longer miss them. You will have defeated that part of the cigarette complex already—easily and comfortably.

Each smoker's tic is unique to himself, different in at least some ways from all other smokers'. Study your own tic with care. As you smoke your next few cigarettes,

The Smoker's Tic

notice every movement you make. Then deliberately change your entire smoking pattern, change every movement, change everything about your method of smoking that you recognize as familiar.

Change brands. Switch to a brand of cigarettes that you have seldom or never smoked before. It should be a brand that is as dissimilar as possible to what you're used to smoking. If you've been using filter tips, switch to an unfiltered brand—or vice versa. Switch from plain to mentholated, from flip-top box to soft pack, from king size to regular size.

Buy cigarettes at unfamiliar places. Never again buy them at the familiar cigar stand on your way to work or at your friendly neighborhood drugstore. From now on, deliberately avoid those places as sources of cigarettes. Otherwise, when you finally reach the Zero Line, you will miss those places and will be reminded of cigarettes every time you pass by. Start weaning yourself now. Seek out new sources of cigarettes, places you've seldom or never visited before. Not just one place: you may get too familiar with it after a while. Seek new sources all the time. If you're used to buying cigarettes in stores, buy them from coin machines whenever possible. If you've generally bought cartons, stop that practice and buy single packs from now on.

Put your cigarettes in a new place. If you've been keeping them in a pocket or handbag, abandon the practice.

Put them on a kitchen shelf, or in a desk drawer. The act of reaching or pocket-dipping for cigarettes is among the most tic-like in the whole array of smokers' movements. From now on, don't allow yourself to go through this movement in your old way. And don't simply switch your cigarettes to a different pocket. Put them in a place where they aren't quite as easy to get at.

One Smoke Watcher even went so far as to put his cigarettes in locked drawers in his home and office. When he wanted to smoke, he had to stand up, get a key, and unlock the drawer. "It was a nuisance," he recalls, "but it got me out of the habit of dipping in my shirt pocket. First few days I found myself dipping in my pocket all the time, like my arm was being run by some machine instead of me. There'd be a funny kind of disoriented feeling when I'd find no cigarettes in the pocket. It was like suddenly waking up from a dream. But after a week I was over it. My arm quit pocket-dipping."

Make it hard to get a cigarette from the pack. The act of extracting a cigarette is another tic-like motion. Some smokers shake a cigarette out, some fumble in the pack with two fingers, some pull out a cigarette with their lips. Whatever your tic has been, force yourself to change.

There are many possible ways of doing this. One is to wrap the pack with rubber bands in such a way that you must unwind them before you can get a cigarette. Another is to wrap your rating form around the pack. Another is to slide off the cellophane wrapping from the pack and replace it upside-down, fitting it over the top

The Smoker's Tic

of the pack like a lid, so that you must remove it before you can get a cigarette.

Still more complicated ideas have been tried by various Smoke Watchers. One woman, every time she bought a new soft pack, would empty out half the cigarettes and flatten the empty side and fasten it with a safety pin. A man of our acquaintance, when he reached a level of about ten cigarettes a day, took to cellophane-taping his day's supply to the inside of his pants leg each morning. "To get a cigarette, I had to take my pants off. It was so much trouble that I went down to the Zero Line after three days."

Change your way of lighting up. If you've been using a lighter, abandon it and switch to matches. If you're right-handed, hold the matchbook in your right hand and strike the match with your left. You'll find it awkward—which is, of course, the whole idea. Don't ever again revert to your old, automatic series of lighting-up motions.

Hold your cigarette in a new way. If you have habitually held the cigarette in one particular hand, switch deliberately to the other. If you've been an ambidextrous smoker, using either hand indiscriminately, you must change to different fingers or a different kind of grip.

One ambidextrous smoker settled on a plan of smoking with his left hand only, holding the cigarette awkwardly between the middle and ring fingers. To force himself to do this (and also to give curious observers a satisfactory explanation of why he was doing it), he bandaged together his index and middle fingers, the ones he had habitually used. Another ambidextrous smoker, a woman, took to using a cigarette holder.

Change your lip grip. If you have changed your way of holding the cigarette, you'll probably find you have to insert it in your mouth from a different angle or at a different point from what you've been used to. If this doesn't happen by itself, force it to happen. Put the cigarette in a new corner of your mouth.

Change your ashtray system. Don't keep ashtrays conveniently next to your favorite chairs or on your desk. Put them all away in a cupboard. From now on, instead of using an ashtray, use a saucer or a paper cup with a little water in the bottom. This will help you convince yourself that you are only a smoker temporarily; you will not need ashtrays much longer. It will also help break your smoker's tic. When you want to smoke, it will be necessary for you to get up and hunt for a makeshift ash receptacle.

Some Smoke Watchers have carried this idea to seemingly ridiculous (but useful) extremes. One man took to using beer and soda bottles as ash receptacles. "It was hard to get the ashes into the narrow mouth of the bottle," he explained. "It wasn't like the old method I used to have, tapping ashes into a big ashtray at my elbow. I'd been a nervous tapper; I was always tapping a cigarette. It was a major part of my physical habit. By forcing myself to use bottles, I got rid of this nervous tic."

Another client, a housewife, smoked at home by spreading a wet paper towel on a countertop in her

The Smoker's Tic

kitchen. "I used the towel as my ashtray. I found the sight and smell of those soggy ashes very distasteful. Sometimes I couldn't wait to finish the damned cigarette and roll up the towel and throw the mess away. Toward the end, I got so disgusted that I'd often throw out the cigarette after I'd taken only a few puffs. The cigarette would start as a Number 5 but end as 1. I think this was the deathblow to my habit, the thing that finally killed it."

. . .

It's up to you to study your own smoking complex and identify all the tic-like components of it. No two smokers' habits are exactly the same—a fact that we Smoke Watchers try never to forget. We have deliberately kept our approach highly flexible, encouraging each smoker to distill our thinking in his own mind and apply it to his habit in whatever way he thinks will be the most effective. Using a wet paper towel as an ashtray may not help you much, and we have no intention of selling this particular notion to you or anybody else. If you think it will help, fine. If not, develop some other device that will be suitable in your specific campaign. As in all phases of the campaign, of course, you should talk over the problem with your fellow campaigners.

This much we're sure of: you must attack your smoker's tic while you are still smoking. The tic must be dead before the rest of this multi-armed complex will die easily.

15 🌲 Extra Ingredients

As you drop down toward the Zero Line, you may feel the need for some extra ingredient to insert into your life in place of cigarettes. It may be an oral substitute—something to put in your mouth. It may be some kind of physical activity to take your mind off cigarettes and dissipate excess energy. It may be a hobby. It may be something else, or a combination.

Whatever extra ingredient attracts you, latch onto it. *But be sure you approach it in the right way.* If you don't, you may damage your campaign and perhaps defeat it entirely.

The idea of a "substitute" to put in your mouth or an activity to "keep you occupied" is among the oldest in the whole encyclopedia of how-to-stop-smoking clichés. Smokers who take the cold-turkey route, especially, strongly feel an emptiness or hole in their lives. They suffer through long periods and perhaps whole days and weeks when they don't quite know what to do with themselves. It seems entirely logical in a situation like this to seek something that can be jammed into the hole, something that will fill the emptiness.

It is logical up to a point. The main danger in it is that it reflects a negative approach—the approach we warned

Extra Ingredients

against in Chapter 7. The act of seeking a "substitute" implies that something good has been taken away. It implies "quitting" rather than moving forward to a bright new life.

This may seem like hairsplitting. Believe us, it isn't. In this business of wrestling with the tobacco complex, your attitude is enormously important. After all, what are we dealing with here but your thoughts and feelings? As we've seen, tobacco is physically addictive only to a minuscule extent, if at all. We aren't wrestling with any physical force. We are up against psychological forces exclusively. Thus, success or failure will be dictated solely by what goes on in your mind. A seemingly minor problem such as a self-defeating attitude toward "substitutes" could easily tip the balance against you.

Millions of smokers have tried to break the habit. The vast majority have failed. They've failed because of psychological factors *alone*.

. . .

To appreciate the dangers in searching for "substitutes," consider the story of Mrs. Clare B., thirty-three, who came to Smoke Watchers after three unsuccessful attempts to succeed in her fourteen-year smoking career. In her last attempt, she had followed advice given in a magazine article.

"I guess I'd enjoyed smoking without regrets or fears until I was in my middle twenties," she told us. "Then I began to get worried about it and disgusted with myself for continuing to smoke. I tried to break the habit on my own twice—once after a bout with pneumonia—and failed both times without really putting up much of a fight. Then, one day, I picked up one of those little health magazines—you know, the kind with fad diets and advertisements for mail-order medicines that are supposed to cure all your ills. One of the articles in the magazine was on how to stop smoking. It was written by somebody I never heard of, a woman. She wasn't identified in any way except by her name. No credentials were given, nor anything to prove she knew any more about smoking than I did. I was foolish to believe what she said. But I wanted to believe it because I was looking for an easy way out of the tobacco trap."

The "easy way" suggested in the article apparently hinged mainly on chewing gum and taking long walks. The article writer urged her readers to take three long walks a day, breathing deeply and filling the lungs with what she called "natural electricity." (She didn't explain what this was or precisely what it was supposed to do.) Furthermore, the readers were counseled to chew up several packs of gum a day, spitting out the old gum and starting a new stick each time they felt the wish for a cigarette.

Clare B. didn't particularly like gum, but she religiously followed the article-writer's advice. "I'd heard other smokers say that chewing gum and taking walks were good substitutes, good ways to keep your mind occupied. So, in a way, it seemed to make sense despite all that weird stuff about 'natural electricity.' I did everything the article said. I chewed gum until my jaws ached, and in fact I developed a toothache the second day. I walked until I thought I'd glow in the dark with natural electricity."

The trouble was, the idea of "quitting" was strongly

Extra Ingredients

implanted in her mind. The gum was a substitute for something good that she was giving up. The walks were a way of taking her mind off her unhappiness. "Every time I put a stick of gum in my mouth, I wished it were a cigarette instead. I kept thinking, 'This is awful. Will I have to do this all my life?' I got so I hated gum and walking, really hated them. And after a week or so, I went back to smoking."

. . .

Her attitude was wrong. *Never* think of a thing as a "substitute," be it candy or a hobby or walking. The word "substitute" carries a connotation of inferiority: something less good than the original. Think, instead, that you are adding an extra ingredient to your life, something that you would not or could not have enjoyed if you had continued smoking.

Never count on any such extra ingredient to "wean" you from smoking. It can't happen that way. The weaning is being accomplished mainly by group pressures and other forces that we've discussed. The extra ingredients you choose, whatever they may be, will contribute to the process in various ways—but no smoker should count on them to carry a major part of the burden. You *can't* succeed against tobacco simply by trying to switch your habituation to something else.

We have deliberately placed this chapter late in the book because we wanted you to get your freedom campaign well established before you began thinking too much about substitutes. You should be somewhere in the range between twenty cigarettes a day and the Zero

THE TECHNIQUES OF SUCCESS

Line before you start applying these principles in earnest. With zero in sight, you can begin to think of ways to bring new experiences into your life.

Each smoker must choose his own. Here are some possibilities—the extra ingredients we've heard Smoke Watchers mention most often:

Oral rewards: Gum, candy, fruit, and other foods. As your level of smoking decreases, your sense of taste will improve markedly. You'll suddenly find that all your favorite foods and drinks taste better. You may not have enjoyed gum, candy, or fruit while you were smoking heavily, partly because you couldn't taste them well, partly because their tastes and tobacco's interfered with each other. A cigarette smoked after chewing a mint gum or eating a sharp-flavored candy or tart fruit doesn't taste good to many smokers, and for that reason—until now—you've avoided gum and candy and fruit. You may remember having enjoyed them as a youngster, but you haven't enjoyed them since. All right: try them now. You may find the experience delightful. Suddenly, you've won back an enjoyable taste.

Don't make the mistake Clare B. made. Don't latch onto some substance like gum and doggedly chew it whether you enjoy it or not, hoping to make it into a cigarette substitute. The oral reward you choose—if you choose any—should be something distinctly enjoyable. It should be a reward, not an exercise in self-denial. Experiment a little. Try foods you used to enjoy before you smoked. Or try a kind of candy you never tasted before.

A word about weight gain. You've probably heard that smokers often gain some weight after coming free. In a

Extra Ingredients

later chapter we'll discuss this phenomenon more fully, but for the moment we can tell you that you probably needn't worry about it too much. If you are worried about it, you can stick to nonfattening oral rewards. Few fruits are fattening. Even a dozen hard candies have little more caloric content than a single slice of buttered toast.

Sports: As your taste returns, so will a good deal of physical energy. Your blood circulation will improve rapidly. Your breathing will become more efficient: your lungs will absorb more oxygen from each breath as their coating of tobacco deposits disappears and as the mucus generated in your bronchial tubes (your body's self-protective device against smoke) subsides. Once again you'll be able to enjoy sports as you did when you were younger.

Don't take up any sport in a spirit of self-denial or asceticism, grimly going through its motions whether you enjoy it or not. This will defeat your purpose. Pick a sport or sports that you find highly enjoyable. Or pick any form of exercise: walking, gardening.

This will in fact have the effect of "keeping your mind occupied," as the cliché goes. But don't think of that as the main purpose. Think instead how much you're enjoying this activity that has newly entered your life. Look ahead to a lifetime of similar pleasures, an enriched existence. And notice, at the same time, how your feeling of fitness is steadily increasing.

Hobbies: Adults often complain that they don't have time for hobbies any more. Often—maybe always—the actual fact is that they lack energy, not time. This is certainly true of the typical smoker. At the end of a day he is too tired to do more than drag his weary way homeward and flop down before a television set and smoke himself into a restless sleep.

As you approach the Zero Line, you will find yourself more energetic after five o'clock and on weekends. You may interpret this faintly jumpy feeling as a withdrawal symptom; you feel you're nervous and irritable because you're without cigarettes. This may be true to a certain extent, but in larger measure the jumpy feeling is actually a symptom of abruptly increased energy. It feels odd because you've been so long without it. You're so used to being tired, "smoked out," that the feeling of bounce and energy comes as a surprise.

You suddenly find yourself with a lot of energy and nowhere to channel it. You aren't used to feeling this good; for years you haven't had this strong urge to do something interesting or creative or constructive. All right: don't be overwhelmed by the feeling. Go back to some of the hobbies or interests that absorbed you when you were younger. For years the thought of pursuing these interests has bored you. Now you may find, to your surprise, that you're hugely interested and absorbed once again.

One client of ours had been a coin collector when he was a younger man. He hadn't looked at his collection for about fifteen years; his mountings and packets of coins and books had been stowed away in an old trunk in his attic. As he approached the Zero Line he began to think about his coins again, and one night he went up to the attic and unpacked the trunk.

"I was up until four the next morning, looking